AF422051

THE SCORPION EFFECT

A GUIDE TO NARCISSISTIC ABUSE

GEORGE E. KELLOGG, MSSM

The Scorpion Effect: A Guide to Narcissistic Abuse
George E. Kellogg, MSSM

All rights reserved
Copyright © 2023 by George E. Kellogg, MSSM

No part of this publication may be reproduced, distributed, or transmitted in any form or by any means, including photocopying, recording, or other electronic or mechanical methods, without the prior written permission of the publisher, except in the case of brief quotations embodied in critical reviews and certain other noncommercial uses permitted by copyright law.

Published by BooxAi
ISBN: 978-965-578-567-8

CONTENTS

INTRODUCTION

This book was written to educate people. It is the author's experienced opinion that all of us should become educated on narcissistic behavior. The author intends to present a warning to the world while entertaining the reader. This is a tricky ambition at best.

We all must learn about narcissism. Like it or not, we will all have to deal with it in life. Encounters with narcissists may occur in family relationships, romance, business, school, and even religious or spiritual organizations. You will also meet narcissists in your local charitable, activist, fraternal, or sorority organizations. It is unavoidable.

It is important to note that we are starting to hear the term "narcissist" strewn about all over the place. Not everyone using the word fully understands the depth of actual narcissism. Too many folks think that when someone carelessly upsets them, or if someone does something selfish, then that makes the offender a narcissist. This reflects a very shallow understanding of the topic.

Granted, narcissism is selfishness. However, *when a person does a selfish thing, that alone does not make them a narcissist.* None of us are perfect. All of us can be selfish. Anyone who has dealt with a child in their "terrible twos" understands this. Certainly, all of us remember our selfish teenage years!

We need to understand that narcissism goes much deeper than just human selfishness. It goes far beyond merely being careless with another's feelings. It is certainly important to address these human faults, but we must do so in an informed manner. We need to be restrained in labeling one or another as a "narcissist" over mere imperfection. Casting the term "narcissistic" onto every selfish act dilutes the meaning of the word. Such dilution diminishes the seriousness of narcissistic abuse. It blinds us to how destructive narcissism is.

Remember how the word "awesome" used to be applied to things like the Grand Canyon, the Great Wall of China, or the Moon Landing? Then in the 80's, everything changed with the nationwide adoption of Valley Girl slang. Now "awesome" is used to describe anything we find favorable. "You brought pizza? *Awesome!*" We see here how the overuse of a word can weaken the importance of its meaning. We don't want to do this with the word "narcissism".

It is the goal of this book to explain in layman's terms what narcissism is. Written here is a brutally honest and in-your-face explanation of narcissism, the behavior of narcissists, and the damage they do to people's lives. The suggestions and ideas presented in this book are not to be used as medical or self-help advice. The author intends to inform the reader and encourage people who have been harmed by narcissistic behavior to find help.

In this book, by the way, the author refers to the narcissist as a "narce". This is an irregular way of abbreviating the word "narcissist". Most of the time you will hear the abbreviation of "narc" in videos, lessons, or literature about narcissists. Nevertheless, in some circles, the term "narc" is slang for one who tells on someone else. "Rat" or "snitch" are used interchangeably with "narc". "Narc" was derived from street slang for "narcotics officers" who enforce drug laws. Using the term "narce" prevents any misunderstandings of the topic at hand.

The author hopes that whatever your reason for picking up this book, you finish reading it and apply what you learn. How can you know if this book is for you? Well, if you have made it this far, then there probably is something of value for you in these pages.

Best of luck and may the Creator prosper your righteous endeavors!

PROLOGUE

This book was written as dictated by a very wise frog.

AND SO, we begin…

I was fishing one day, minding my own business, as usual. It was a warm summer day with blue skies and puffy white clouds. I was fishing at an Ohio farm pond, typical to rural Ohio. I was very content that day, fishing as I sat on a large stone wheel from some historical grist mill. The stone wheel lay at the water's edge and was the perfect place upon which to sit and fish.

The channel catfishes in this particular pond were quite sizable, and catching one was like trying to haul a log out of a foot of sticky mud. A bite would have meant work catching the cussed fish, or cutting the line and losing valuable tackle. Neither option was very attractive to me on this warm summer day with blue skies and puffy white clouds. I was content to just be there, doing nothing.

An old bullfrog sat languidly nearby, on top of a patch of moss. He would have fallen through the moss, but he had partially inflated so he could just sit there. He was minding his own business, too. Or at least I thought he was. As he sat there quietly, his eyes never left me, but that seemed pretty normal for a frog. The thought never emerged that he just might be *observing* me.

Then out of nowhere, I heard a throaty voice: "You shouldn't do that you know."

Needless to say, I nearly jumped out of my own skin! In fact, I did leap to my feet immediately, being kind of a jumpy guy by nature. Mother Nature was a hard teacher and she had wired into me an exaggerated "fight or flight" reflex. I was ready to fight because it seemed that I was being approached from behind by an unseen stranger. I knew that being this close to the water put me at risk of being shoved into the pond.

I was startled because rural Ohio has its share of pranksters, too. One never knows when some jerk might be half-drunk and ready to kick a fellah into a pond for minding his own business! That's a good way to lose fishing gear, too, because the prankster might just have his eye on your fishing pole. My pole was a particularly nice, custom-made rod. Very expensive.

I looked around and saw no one. I was surrounded by an open, grassy field and some horses that were behind a rubber-strap fence. So, I went back to minding my own business, with the frog still there. Then I heard the same throaty voice: "Jumpy little fish, aren't you?" I was not as startled this time because I was getting used to hearing the voice. The voice's familiarity, however, did very little to settle my mind. After all, no one likes to contend with the idea that they are hearing disembodied voices.

"All right, just what the heck is going on here?" I asked out loudly.

"Are you talking to me, or just talking to yourself again? You should not do that, you know."

"Do what?" I asked, still looking around me.

"Talk to yourself. I know that it does not mean you are nutty or anything. But someone who does not understand human nature like I do will think you are off your rocker."

"Well, then, whoever you are, show yourself."

"I am showing myself. You have looked at me several times."

"Very funny. Where are you hiding? Who sent you to mess with me?"

"Well, you are half right. Sent, yes. Messing with you, no."

"Well, 50 percent is still a failing grade, mister!"

"How clever. You have been to college, then? Please say 'yes'."

"I have been to college, yes. I have... wait, no, if you don't show me who you are right now, I won't say another word. It is none of your business where I've been."

I looked in the direction of the voice and saw the frog. *Then the frog looked me straight in the eye.* That was quite unsettling, being *stared in the eye* by an amphibian. I could sense, definitely, that this amphibian was no mere "frog". This was some kind of sentient being, and he was studying me, sizing me up. All I could do was stare while the frog took control of the situation.

"I would not tell a stranger my business, either. It's not safe. But know that you are safe with me. I am your friend. You may call me Frog. I am, in case you were wondering, a male frog," he said.

"I see," I responded, even though I did not see. Not at all.

"I know that you do not see. Your 'I see' was a throwaway phrase that you used to close a gap in the conversation. Wasn't it?"

He had me there. "Yes."

"Fear not, George, because you will soon see."

"See what?"

"Your life in a whole new way. That persistent fog in your mind will clear and your heart will begin to mend."

"How, Frog? How do you know about the fog and my broken heart? Is there some magic about you?"

"'Magic' is the word you use to describe a miracle you don't understand. But you also use it to describe a sleight-of-hand trick. The distance between the two creates quite a broad spectrum. Where do you think I lie in that spectrum? Am I a miracle or a cheap parlor trick?"

"Swim for me. Show me that you are a frog, Frog."

"Very well." He swam and went underwater, then he returned and hopped out of the water, onto the millstone. I was sitting down now, so he hopped onto my leg. "Touch me," he instructed.

So, I did. I poked him with one finger, ran that finger across his moist hide, and knew that he was a real frog.

"Satisfied?" he asked me.

"Satisfied, Frog. I am satisfied."

"All right, now that you are satisfied, what do we do about it?"

"Do about it?"

"You are satisfied that I am a real, talking frog. What do you intend to do with me? I am in your hands and you are much larger than me. You can do whatever you like with me. Are you going to capture me, take me home, and eat my tender legs? Are you going to sell me to the circus? Put me on the Internet? What? What are you going to do now?"

"I don't know what to do, but I do know that I will not harm you."

"There's a good fellow. I'm glad we got that out of the way."

"Somehow, I think that harming you would result in greater harm to me," I said in partial amazement, but with great conviction.

"Yes, it would. I am not an ordinary frog. Not only can I talk, but I made a special deal with Our Creator.

"A *deal?* What kind of deal could a *frog* make with *God?*"

"Our Creator spared my life. And in exchange, I have been commissioned to travel the world and warn people."

"Warn people? About what?"

"Before I start to tell you, maybe we should go over a few things."

Well, naturally, by now I was completely taken by this situation. Frog had all of my attention. After all, how often does one come by a talking frog at the local farm pond? We hear about them in fairy tales but we never consider in our real lives that animals, much less frogs, can talk. Even if they did talk, what could they say that would be of importance to us humans?

Though I knew that a frog couldn't talk, I did know that God makes miracles sometimes and, well, if this was one of them, I should pay attention. If it all turned out that this was just a dream, then it was a funny one I could share with people. Not only that but if I woke up from the dream, and the frog was still there, I could capture him and cook him up! So, really, what did I have to lose by listening?

That one decision changed the course of my entire life.

1

THE FROG'S STORY

By now, I knew that my day of fishing had ended. *I was conversing with a frog.* He somehow knew my name and now I knew his. This was a male frog, who preferred to be called "Frog." I was conversing with him, which seemed impossible. Yet, I did not believe that I was losing my mind. Since my fishing had ended, I went ahead and stowed my gear properly and placed it on the bank beside me. Then I settled in to hear the frog's tale.

"So, George, let me tell you how I became who I am. You're probably wondering if I am a human who became a frog. Your fairy tales and lore have taught you that from the crib. With patience, you will realize that I am a talking frog of great experience. Please understand that I am immortal, after a fashion, but I am not human. I speak in man tongues because I was granted the gift of tongues by the Creator.

"I have heard of that, 'the gift of tongues', but what is it?" I asked in earnest.

"Well, the gift of tongues allows you to hear my native croaking language in English. Before you ask, yes, I have visited other lands as well. Chinese speakers hear me in Chinese. Germans hear me in German. Bi or Multi-lingual people hear me in whichever tongue is easiest for them. Sometimes they hear me in a mixture of tongues. It does not matter to me what language they hear, as long as they understand what I say."

"That, Frog, is fascinating! I am… overwhelmed."

"As you should be."

"So… if anyone walks by, will they hear you in their tongue?"

"Only if they are meant to hear me. Most likely, anyone who passes by us will only see you talking to a croaking frog. Without exception, they will continue walking and not even ask what you are doing. They would rather not know!"

That made me chuckle. "Everyone I know around here realizes that I have a habit of talking to myself, so they would think nothing of me sitting here talking to you, Frog."

"Yes, these folks have a reputation for minding their own business."

"They do, yes. At least they do once they graduate high school. The teen social scene here is a nightmare."

"The teen scene has always been a nightmare, all over the world. Juvenile thinking is the same across the globe. We are about to discuss the problems caused by adults who never grew past that type of thinking. Now, George, it is time to get down to business. Are you familiar with the fable of *The Frog and the Scorpion* at all?"

"I am not."

"I will review it, then. There once was a frog, that was me. One day a scorpion approached me. We were on the bank of a river, its location is not important, and I jumped onto a rock out in the water to escape harm. I knew scorpions to be deadly with their stinging tails. After I landed on the rock, the scorpion spoke to me. Don't ask me how, just know that he did. Are you with me so far, George?"

"Yes, so far. Please go on."

"Well, the scorpion asked me to not hop away from him. There was a certain food supply that he needed. I never learned what it was, or if such food even existed, but whatever the case, he said he had run out of food. He claimed that he was starving to death. The food was supposedly on the other side of the river. Naturally, I did not trust the scorpion. They had a reputation for being rather mean and dangerous. I did not want to get near enough for him to sting me. Got it?"

"Yes. I get it. The sting would paralyze or kill you."

"Right. Very good. So, the scorpion told me that all he needed was a ride to the other side of the river. He could not swim, naturally, so he needed a swimming creature to carry him across the river. I resisted and said that I would not carry him on my back. I suggested he talk to a turtle with a hard shell to protect itself."

"That was a good idea."

"Yes, it was, but the scorpion insisted that the turtles would just draw in their legs and heads and not talk to him when he tried to ask. The turtles, you see, did not want to be stung. So, even if a turtle did offer a ride, the scorpion feared that the turtle get scared halfway across, retreat into its shell, sink and the scorpion would drown."

"A reasonable presumption."

"Indeed. Well, I began to converse with the scorpion, sensing the desperation of his plight. Once he had me as an audience, he began to explain how he was no ordinary scorpion. His outer colors were beautiful. His claws were very powerful. He was strong, clever, and a credit to his race. He could not allow his race to go without him, as he was too important."

"I see. Then what?"

"He began to tell me that he understood the noble character of the Frog race. He was fascinated by Frogs and loved to study them and converse with them. He said he believed that Frogs were valuable; we were far too precious to harm. He thought that the Frog race was at the same level as the Scorpion race. He thought that I was brilliant enough to be valuable to his people. I could be the one to help unite the Frog and Scorpion kingdoms. He knew that no harm would come to me if I delivered him safely. The Scorpion community would embrace me as a friend and even a hero because I saved their most valued member."

"That must have been quite flattering, to be considered so special, Frog."

"Oh, yes, it was. It was most flattering. The scorpion continued to tell me that not only was he important to the perpetuation of his community, but I was just as important because I could save his life. I would be a hero to his kind. Not only would I have Scorpion praise and adulation, but he and I would be responsible for beginning Frog/Scorpion relations that would last throughout the generations to follow. Praise and honor would be shed upon me and my family for generations to come. I would ever be venerated. I not only listened but I was greatly influenced by his kind words and captivating charisma. I was fascinated by the visions of grandeur and the joyful picture he was painting for me."

"Yes, about anyone would be captivated by such an offer."

"Indeed. It was a very tempting pitch. Even so, something did not seem right. I could not put my finger on what might be wrong, though. Despite my misgivings, I continued to listen to the scorpion. As he continued to talk, I became more and more convinced of his sincerity. I did not realize it at the time, but he was simply repeating himself over and over again. He was reciting the same ideas, but using different words. He never deviated from his message, but he chose his words intentionally. He gauged my reactions to his words. He paid close attention to my body language. He would pick the expressions that were the most influential to my mind. He changed his voice's pitch, tone, and timbre to that which was most pleasing to me. He was a very good salesman."

"Yes, a salesman is what he was, Frog. You are describing the perfect salesman. He used the words and tones of voice that made you trust him. He put you 'under the ether', in salesman parlance. He used a form of manipulation to make you feel good. He wanted you to think you were working in your best interest, to buy or do something he was selling or promoting. You were convinced, while under the ether, that this thing would make you happy. Often, when humans are under the ether, they won't even realize what they did until the next day. By then, it is too late. The deal is done and they are stuck with the consequences, usually in the form of a payment they cannot afford."

"You are correct, George. I was about to buy something that I could not afford. In my case, I bought what the scorpion was selling. The price of giving someone a tow across the river was small for the benefits that he was touting to me. After all, who would not want to save a life and then have praise and honors sung to his name long after he was dead? Who would not want to foster relations between natural enemies and unite two communities into a wonderful organization that would last forever? I was sold on this whole idea with delightful pictures running through my mind."

We agreed that I would give the scorpion passage across the river. He would have his food supply. His life would be saved. In exchange, I would receive all the benefits, praise, and honors of being a hero. Together would unite Scorpion and Frog communities. We would organize a kingdom of beneficial interest for all concerned parties. It was the perfect deal."

"And the deal turned out how?"

"The way that you believe it did. I demanded a final assurance from Scorpion that he would not sting me and drown us both. He promised again that he would not sting me. After all, where is the benefit for him in doing so? Customarily, yes, he would sting a frog just to be mean, but his hunger gave him a change of heart. He had no desire to starve, no desire to drown, and he had only the best of intentions for both of us. We were to have the praise and honor of the Frog/Scorpion world. I was finally convinced; my initial misgivings were washed away. I bought his grand vision."

"Then you gave him the ride." I shook my head and sighed.

"Are you judging me for having compassion and weakness for another living being's plight?"

"I am not judging you. I shook my head because your story is so very common."

"Good. I was hoping you would understand. Now to finish the story. I returned to Scorpion and sat in the water as he climbed onto my back. I told him to hold tight because if he fell off, the river would sweep him away and I would not be able to help. He said he knew that he would certainly drown if he fell, so yes, he would hold tight. Once he was securely aboard, I swam out into the river. My hind legs kicked us along powerfully. This trip was familiar. I had made the journey many times. I would easily get my new friend across the river in about twenty minutes and what a great time we would have!"

"Well, you did not see where things could go wrong, but I think they did."

"You are correct, George. Scorpion and I got along very well for the first half of our crossing. We laughed and carried on, rejoicing in our friendship. But then… Scorpion started to talk about the faults of the Frog race, and how he was a superior being of a race that was of a higher class than mine. This began to irritate me. Then I thought better of it, making the excuse that things could not always go smoothly. There were bound to be bumps in the road when forming a friendship with a natural enemy.

I casually defended the Frog race, speaking of the virtues and natural compassion of our kind. Then he asked why, if I was so innocent, would I be willing to listen to a Scorpion. After all, everyone understands that a Scorpion is a devious creature. I responded that he and I were friends and I was trying to save his life.

He scoffed at me. "Sounds like things were coming apart."

"They were, and very quickly, too. Soon, he started telling me Scorpions were always going to be better than Frogs, no matter what. He accused me of trying to take advantage of him for all the gifts he could give me. He told me that he was doing me a favor by trying to reach down and lift me. Scorpion said that he knew the only reason I was helping him was so that I could take advantage of him later.

"I tried to defend myself and my race, not believing how Scorpion was lambasting me and the other Frogs. After all, I was the very Frog who was trying to save his life. Then he continued accusing me of trying to take advantage of him. He said that I convinced him to introduce me to his race for personal gain. He said I was leveraging his starvation against him. He said that he knew that I was only helping him to get advantages for myself. He claimed that he knew that I was taking advantage of him.

"When I recollected to him that he was the one who made the offer of uniting our races and giving me praise and honor, he became angry. How dare I challenge him and say that he, the superior representative of the superior Scorpion race, was wrong? Why would he make such an offer to such an unworthy, inferior being of an inferior race? Why, he even said that I was about the lowest Frog he ever met!

"All of this while you were laboring for him, to save his life."

"Yes. Then, finally, when he objected to my reminding him of how he praised me just moments ago, he became livid! He said that he would prove to me how stupid I was. He would prove to me, and everyone, that I was very stupid. No Frog in his right mind would help a Scorpion. That was when he stung me! Now, had there been just the one sting, I would have been able to save us."

"That was not the case though."

"You may have already guessed how it ends, but I must finish the story. In his rage, he did not sting me once out of anger and immediately regret it or apologize. No, he stung me many times and berated me. He cursed my ancestry and hollered about how my past was nothing, my present was just being a stupid Frog, and he would make sure that I had no future."

"But he would have no future, either…"

"I am getting to that and I am glad you are keeping up on the story. I cannot describe how terrible it felt, to get punished for doing the right thing. While the promises of glory and honor were attractive, at the end of the day, I just wanted to help a fellow sentient creature. Scorpion, though, was not just upset. He was terribly spiteful about the whole thing. He was getting 'revenge' on an innocent, fellow creature who had done nothing but good for him.

"His twisted reason for revenge was because I dared help a Scorpion. I, a stupid low-life idiotic Frog, allowed myself to be fooled. I was inferior; therefore, I deserved whatever punishment Scorpion should allocate to me."

"So, if revenge was the goal, why not wait until the two of you reached the other side?" I asked, very interested now.

"That would be the reasonable thing, wouldn't it? The problem was that Scorpion was already filled with self-doubt and shame. He may have had beautiful colors and a powerful body, but he really did not believe in himself. He was actually ashamed of himself and all of his confidence was a front. He had charisma and wonderful ideas, but he secretly hated himself and never carried through on anything valuable or productive.

"When he knew that I genuinely cared for him, he decided to take revenge on me. He was so self-repulsed that he made the choice that we both deserved to die. All because he did not believe that he was worthy of my friendship."

"So… he killed you both? But you are here, alive…"

"We will come to that in a moment… As to my passing, the stings in my flesh were not as painful as you might think, but when the venom reacted with my muscles and nerves, it burned like fire. Then I went cold and became numb. In another moment, I was on fire all over again. Finally, my body locked up and went into shock. I rolled over in the water. Naturally, Scorpion could not hang on. I saw that he was being carried away by the river.

"I had a dying conversation with Scorpion. I asked him why he did this. He said, 'Frog, it is just who I am and I don't regret what I did. But you should be ashamed because this is your fault. You were the one who was stupid enough to trust me. I gave you only what you deserved.' The last I saw of him, he was lamenting that the Scorpion race would be denied his beauty and it was the fault of the Frog race."

"That made no sense."

"Correct. But, as you know, that is not the end of the story. I was floating belly up. I was trying to kick with my legs, but they only twitched and convulsed. Then I heard a calm, kind voice. The voice said that I was valiant and did the right thing. The voice said I did not have vengeance and anger in my heart, even as I was dying at the hands of an enemy, whom I trusted and loved. I asked the voice who it was. 'I am the Creator' was all it said. I asked the Creator to be merciful and take me quickly.

"The Creator said that this could be done, but if I would rather live, there was a job for me to do. If I chose to do so, I would travel the world under the power of the Creator's hand. I was to tell the story of The Frog and the Scorpion to valiant but deprived souls who would listen. If I were so willing, the Creator would allow me to remain on Earth and I would not have to experience the terrors of death. This would be my reward for the purity of my motives and actions. It was my choice, now. Immediately, I felt that I wanted to help others avoid my fate. I took my second deal of the day, only this time it was the right one."

"I see… So are you now like John the Immortal, who travels the world, seeking to minister to mankind?"

"Yes. I am Frog, the Immortal. Don't laugh. That's what they named me, in Frog tongue, of course."

"Of course. Okay, then," I said with a smile. "Frog the Immortal it is. So… why are you talking to me?"

"Something you will learn, George, is that I don't pick my material. I just work with what I am handed."

"I'm not sure how to take that," I chuckled, "but I guess that I have been… chosen?"

"Yes. You have been chosen. You have been chosen to write my story, as others have been chosen through the ages. The Frog and Scorpion fable that all of you know came from chosen writers. But now, you as the newly chosen writer, will explain the lesson of the fable. You have been called to write about why others treat people this way. Plus, you are to write something about how to heal the victims' hearts, minds, and lives from such abuse."

"I am not a therapist."

"Good. I don't need a therapist."

"I think I might need one… I've been talking to a frog," I chuckled mildly.

"This late in the conversation, you come up with a quip like that? Look… George… either you are in or you are out. I don't have time for games."

"If I come into this thing, what is the deal?"

"It's very simple. If you say yes and 'come into this thing', as you put it, you write my story and publish it. If you say 'no', which have every right to do, you will awaken on this pond bank and believe it all to be a weird dream. You will continue with your life as though you and I never conversed."

"So, if I understand it correctly, I don't make up the story, I just write it."

"Yes. These stubby arms don't hold a pen very well, and forget trying to reach a word processor."

"I see…" then I pondered a moment.

"Well? What is the answer? Do you think you are the only writer out there? I mean, yes, I have been trying to get someone to work with me since the days of the Gutenberg Press. I would love it if you agreed to answer the call. However, if you say no, I will just continue verbally sharing my story wherever I may and I will keep searching for a writer.

"Honestly, I don't want to spend any more time searching. I want to do this immediately. You telling this story could start certain people on the road to a new understanding of 'narcissistic abuse.' There are already many experts out there talking about this. Everyone responds differently to different words, media, and methods. This is your chance to get the message to people who will be influenced by your particular words."

"All right, Frog," I sighed. "Yes. I will do it. You have a writer. I mean, really, what have I to lose?"

"That's the spirit! Yes! I hoped you would be the one. You will be easier to work with than others I have approached through the ages. Not only have you been a sufferer of these abuses yourself, but you didn't try to kill me like King Henry did, thinking I was bewitched. Dickens dismissed me as an imaginary fabrication 'caused by a fragment of underdone potato or a blot of mustard.' Twain, or Samuel Clemens, was a curmudgeon. He was generally unpleasant. He thought I was a hallucination brought on by 'too much sippin' whiskey.' Bradbury wanted to turn my story into a most fanciful tale about a dystopian Martian world governed by narcissists and an armed rebellion against them. But you, George, if you are willing to tell the story on my terms… I think you might be just the guy."

"Let's hope so. Let's hope people believe my story. A talking frog?"

"Let's hope that they glean from the story what is intended, whether they believe you talked to a frog or not. That will be the purpose of the book, you know."

"Purpose?"

"Yes. To help people understand the true nature of narcissism and/or help them get started on recovery from narcissistic abuse, as applicable."

"Well, how do we start?"

"Go home and write what we have already discussed, and then come back here with a pen and one of your legal pads. We will write a little bit every day that you are available. This mission will not interfere with your mode of living. You will spend spare time writing, instead of pretending to fish."

"Okay. I will come back tomorrow, early in the morning so we can get a decent leg up on things. On workdays, I will come after in the latter part of the afternoon. Wait… how do you know I use legal pads for writing?"

"I have been watching you for a while. Don't ask me how. Now, I have a serious question. If this project stretches into the cold months, can I live with you in a fish tank?"

"You know about fish tanks?"

"Don't be naïve! I have wandered this earth for centuries! You don't think that I have spent all my time in farm ponds talking to dragonflies, do you? They are good company and all… but I have lived in fish tanks when the occasion required it."

"Wow! Where have you been, Frog?"

I have traveled the world. I have seen Greece, Europe, and Asia and I have interviewed some of the world's finest minds. I even met with both Freud and Jung, which was interesting. Jung was more open to me than Freud, who kept referring to me in oddly uncomfortable terms.

"I was present during the Reign of Terror in France, the Great Depression, and your Revolutionary War. I lived in Pennsylvania during the Civil War. I have witnessed many great events including the Moon Landing. Oh, yes, I have seen much. I was near many battlefields in World War I, World War II, Korea, and Vietnam.

"Through all of it has run a common thread of *narcissism*. Terrible is the amount of blood that has been spilled across the world in the name of some narcissist or another. You and I won't be able to stop people from becoming narcissists. However, I believe we certainly can help improve some lives. I hope to stop the shedding of so much blood. Well… I will see you in the morning."

Then Frog hopped into the water and ended our meeting. Just like that, I was left alone to ponder the singularity of it all. I wanted to doubt my own senses, but I learned to not do that long ago. My instincts burned with the reality and enormity of the task I had just been given.

Besides, if did write down the story, and returned the next day with pen and paper in hand, just to discover that this initial meeting was a peculiar derangement, I still had a heck of a story idea. So, really, there was no way to lose. I went home and wrote down all of the things I promised Frog I would write.

2

THE FROG AND THE NEW DEAL

EARLY THE NEXT MORNING, I rolled out of bed. I took a handful of pens and a package of legal pads with me to the pond. I went back to the same spot on the millstone with my back to the trees. It was another clear day and I did not bother to wonder if I had lost my mind. I would find out for certain, soon enough. I sat down in the same spot where I was the day before. It was a quiet morning. The sun was rising and it was beautiful to see it reflect on the pond. Then I heard a croaking noise. I was delighted!

"Morning, Frog!" I exclaimed. "I am ready to get started!"

"Get started on what, George?" I spun around. I saw the man who owned the pond and the land it was on. He was on one of his horses, checking the fences. "You talking to yourself again?"

"Well, Mr. Bryant, you've known me since I was a kid. You and the whole town know that we writers are an odd lot."

"Ha-ha! Yes, George. You are an odd one, but honest. Have a great day on the pond, son. Stay as long as you like," and he rode off.

I waited until Mr. Bryant was out of sight and spoke to Frog again. "So, is that you, Frog? Or do I have the wrong one?" I asked my green, floating friend.

"No, George, it is me," said Frog.

"Gaaahh! Holy jumpin' beans! You're *real*!"

"Yes, I am real. What you wrote was real. We are real. So is your calling. Are you reassured enough now to continue?" Impatience was creeping into his voice, despite his understanding of why I may have doubts.

"Frog! You're real! Yes! Yes, I am ready. I am excited!" I sat down, pen at ready.

"Well, that was a quick recovery! Okay then, let's get started. First, you are at liberty to write this or not, just like all the other writers. It has been frustrating for me to find a writer that will finish this project. I am called by the Creator, yes, but that does not mean I always know what I am doing. The Creator does not always give me instructions. I have to figure most of this out, come up with a plan, and then take it to the Creator for approval. Then I either get approval or sometimes it is back to the lily pad to figure it out. I do my best thinking on lily pads."

"So, the Creator is God."

"You may say that the Creator is God. But I did not tell you so. I know what I know of the Creator. You know what you know of the Creator and we will leave it at that. I am not here to preach religion, or to teach you of the Creator. I am here to teach you about narcissistic abuse. I have only brought up the Creator so that you did not think that I was some kind of alien life form or something. Being created by the same Maker gives us some common ground. This is about the only common ground a man and a frog may have."

"I would say so, yes. Okay, so we have common ground. What now?"

"If you have not already begun writing, do so now. I want to say on paper that this has been very frustrating for me. Having a divine calling does not free one from frustrations. One big frustration has been having a limited ability to teach."

"How do you mean?"

"Well, I cannot exactly lecture at a university or appear on the Internet. I cannot write. I can only appear to one person at a time and teach them. Most of the people I approach, as you can understand, don't appreciate being taught by a frog."

"No, I am sure they don't."

"My frustration has been that I cannot present this material without the help of an author. Remember how I touched on my bad luck at finding writers?"

I nodded, "Yes."

"Well, you are the first author who actually offered to get my words out to the world as I give them to you. To recap what we discussed yesterday, many would not believe I was real, or they wanted to change the story to suit their own marketing plans. On the more positive side, a few writers laid off alcohol and recreational drug use after our meeting."

"I bet they did. But what about holy men, priests, shamans, and the like?"

"They had too many agendas and beliefs already in place. Or they had the desire to keep my teaching as 'sacred' and would only pass it down to so many. These are the kind of people who leaked out that *Frog and Scorpion* parable, but would go no further.

"It is time now to teach not only a moral lesson but to teach how to begin healing. This message is more critical now than it has ever been before! We need to reach more than one person at a time."

"A quick question. I think I know the answer, but have you ever been human?"

"I already said I was not human. Now that you agreed to work with me, you have earned the right to hear my life's story summed up. Listen closely; I am going to say it quickly and I don't want to repeat it. I was hatched as a tadpole, grew into a frog, stayed a frog, and was changed into an immortal frog. I was given the divine mission of teaching people about narcissism. At my mission's end, I will merge into Paradise without tasting true death as a frog. The Creator has a purpose for all of his creatures. Any creature doing the Creator's will goes to Paradise. Just like people."

"Wow. That's wonderful!"

"Puts a whole new slant on life, eh?"

"Yes… This is fascinating. Tell me, did your world travels teach you much?"

"Yes, I have been all over the world, learning that narcissism is as common as sand. Sand exists all over the world and so do narcissistic abusers. I am so glad that I have the gifts I have. I have learned much."

"I bet you have. How many have you taught?"

"Over the many centuries, I have taught thousands because it has been slow going. 'Thousands' sounds like a lot, but not when billions need to learn. With your help, I hope to teach many of those billions."

"Why don't we just put you on the Internet from my place?"

"Well, we would reach a lot of people, but think of the consequences. If we proved I was a real frog, I would suffer all kinds of kidnapping attempts, people trying to turn me into a prince, scientists trying to study me, etc. Or, if I was presented as an animated frog, people wouldn't take me seriously. Besides all that, there is something about print that just attracts people. A hard copy of a book can be passed from hand to hand. People can write notes and insights on the margins. Books are fun and I hope to sell millions of copies."

"I hope we do, too. Is there a problem with selling these teachings?"

"None at all. You deserve to profit from this secular, yet divine, work."

"Very well then," I said. "Let's get started. I would do this for free, actually, but if there are no divine dictates against selling it, I can do that, too."

"All right," said Frog. "We have settled it, then. I dictate to you, you write it down and then do with it as you see fit. I hope you will publish my words to the world."

3

LEARNING THE TERMINOLOGY OF NARCISSISM

"THE FIRST THING you need to know," said Frog, "is that common terminology is needed to teach about narcissism. The world's greatest teachers are also the world's simplest. They keep their teaching understandable to all people. Their words are not for the men in ivory towers who speak wisely but behave foolishly. These words I give you are not exclusive to the educated elite. The truths I am giving you are for all mankind to understand. This book must not be an academic-style text. It must be written for the farmer and the engineer. For the rancher and the orator. For the doctor and the preacher. Do you understand me?"

"Yes."

"Good. Now, in the book, you must put a glossary to explain the terms we're going to discuss. We want students and victims of narcissistic abuse to learn terminology that will allow them to communicate with sort of a code. If words such as 'hoover', 'gray rock', or 'discard' come up in conversation, the student of narcissistic abuse will immediately understand that they are talking to a fellow student, victim, or a survivor of narcissistic behavior."

"May I shorten the term 'narcissistic' to *narce*? I don't like writing that word all the time in its full form."

"Well, yes... don't see why not. Coin that term, but explain it in the glossary."

"I will do that."

"Is there any more you need to know about the terminology?"

"I guess we will cover the words as we get to them."

"We shall. Let's talk now about the personality of the narce and the victim."

"I will write as you talk."

4

THE PREDATOR AND THE PREY

FROG CLEARED the frog in his throat, pun intended. Then, he started the strangest and most off-the-wall lecture series I have ever been audience to before or since. Here I was, breath abated, sitting at Old Man Bryant's pond, *eagerly awaiting the first words of a frog who was centuries old.* It was still hard to believe.

Frog began speaking: "Since we are discussing a human predator, one that will not listen to reason or logic, and who believes they do absolutely no wrong, there is no point in dissecting the narce's personality. This is not an attempt at analysis, or finding a cure for narcissistic personality disorder. We are not going to dig into whether or not the narces, as you like to call them, are born or made."

"Well, why not?" I asked sincerely.

"For our purposes, the origin of the narce will not matter. We are here to teach victims and potential victims. We are here to help people understand that a true narce will not see any reason to change. Because we cannot help them to see their wrongs, we are not interested in where their tendencies come from. I will say that one who has some traits of a narce can change those traits, yes. After all, each of us has a bit of narcissism in us because we all have some selfishness. Sometimes, we need to take stock of our lives. We need to review how we treat others and then adopt a healthier way about us. People can change selfish tendencies."

"All right," I said, "so, why are we not all considered to be narces, if we are selfish by nature?"

"I was about the explain that," said Frog. "A true narce, who is a narce through and through, is rarely capable of changing into a 'normal, empathetic person'. The true narce is not capable of introspection. The last thing a narce wants is to start looking inside because they cannot stand the thought that they are not perfect. They cannot stand to see their own faults. It is too painful for them. This causes them to project or deflect their faults onto other people, blaming others for their narce behaviors. That is all I have to say on that subject, for the moment.

What we want to do right now is to warn the people of what the narce is out to do. We need to pay special attention to those who are the most susceptible to the narce's ways. We want to warn the narce's prey of how the predator works on their mind to keep them under control."

"I see," I said, "I am hearing that there is one particular kind of person that is more easily affected by a narce than others."

"Yes. And this is the personality type that we are going to discuss. I shall say that first of all, these victims are some of the strongest and yet kindest people in the world. These people are always looking out for the other guy. They want the best for everyone involved in any given situation. They want to keep things fair! These people have *empathy* as their primary trait. Practically everything they do is motivated by empathy.

"True *empaths*, as they are called, don't just *meet* people. They *feel* people. Some empaths can actually feel what another person thinks, even when they are a great distance from the person. Not only do they feel what the other person feels, but they also want the best someone else to be happier, healthier, and more successful. Empaths are natural servants and people-pleasers. They are a giving-type person, even to a fault, in many cases. The empath would rather give far too much than fall even a little bit short.

"Though admirable and much needed, empaths are also easily fooled by a narce. This is because the narce knows that *empath* is a people pleaser. They naturally serve. This is the perfect target for a narce. You see, the narce wants to be pleased and continually served. To trap an empath, the narce will actually generate a special false persona. This is a type of mask, that will cause them to appear as a loving person. The narce will generate loving feelings, but the love is not what the empath thinks it is.

"Even if someone tries to warn them, likely, the *empath* will not believe that their true love is manipulating them. This is because the empath will not be able to think in such devious terms. Hopefully, the *empath* will learn of narces from books or other sources that explain the narce's devious mindset. Otherwise, the empath will have to learn hard lessons from experience.

"When the mask slips and it always will, the empath will almost certainly feel a strange or bad vibe from the narce, once or maybe twice. The narce will quickly cover it up and the empath will just as quickly forgive and forget it.

"The empath will probably think that the bad feeling was something they imagined or generated in a moment of weakness. *They do not want to believe that another person can actually fake being in love. They want to believe in the "love bomb" sensation that the narce is putting out. That vibe is strong enough to cover the narce's true intentions, in spite of the mask slipping.*

"This is why the narce's victim is almost always a person of high empathy. *Empaths* will fall into the narce's trap, believing that they have a mutually loving and respectful relationship. The empath will pour their whole soul into trying to make the narce happy. The problem is that the empath, unless otherwise educated, will fail to realize that they cannot please the narce.

"The narce will feign happiness just long enough to draw the empath in. When the narce is finally successful and has hooked their fish, the 'love bombing' suddenly ends. The narce will no longer do over-the-top things to manipulate the empath. The empath, once sold on the narce, has now become the *victim.*

"Since the narce is a user who is more than willing to take all the victim offers, the narce will always take full advantage of the loving, sincere, giving empath every time. The empathic victim will continue to give until they can give no more. In the end, the victim will be completely spent. They will not understand why the narce treated them that way. They will only know that they are both terribly injured and exhausted.

"Even in their exhausted state, it is more than likely that the empath will still try to 'help' the narce. They will try to teach them how to become a better person. The empath will always believe in the narce and will hope that the he or she will change. The victim will have a hard time giving up on the narce. The relationship may end, but the empath will still be open to fixing things, still.

"The *empath*, always trying to do 'the right thing' may even be 'glad to help' with money, food, or whatever the narce requires. It is because the *empath* has a need to be loved, respected, or liked by the narce. The *empath* still believes that there is hope for the relationship, no matter how unreasonable that may be. This is an unhealthy bond between the two, called a 'trauma bond'. It always works to the advantage of the narce. The *empath* never gets the respect or love they deserve and for which they continually strive.

"This type of bonding can last for years. The trauma bond literally will wreck the life of an empath, and only ends when the empath no longer allows him/herself to be abused. We will talk more about trauma bonding later."

"That… Wow. I just don't know what to say. What kind of person does that?" I asked.

"I was just about to explain if you are still up to working."

"I am, Frog."

"Very well then; we shall continue."

5

NARCISSISTIC MOTIVES AND ACTIONS

"Now, we will not spend a lot of time dissecting the narce's personality, but it is necessary to know what motivates them. Bear with me while I go into what motivates every narce and how they will act out.

"We will start by saying that *the narce is all about themselves in all times and all places.* They can excuse themselves for anything and everything. They see everything as a competition to prove they are the best at everything. These people diminish all things, people, and organizations that would prove or say the narce is less than superior. They crave the center of attention more than anything. The spotlight *must* be theirs!

"Being the number one, being the center of attention, and having their every need catered to are not only desires but *cravings.* The narce is attention-starved and they cannot live without the constant praise and support of others. *They will do whatever they must by using whomever they must to satisfy their desires.* They will objectify, vilify, and even demonize anyone who dares to stand up to them. Standing up to the narce causes them offense and injury.

"Offending a narce can mean something as simple as proving them wrong on some minor point during a discussion. It can mean publicly doing something that they, the narce, cannot do. Such things strike a serious blow to their ego, to their false self. They cannot truly be glad for another's achievements. They want all those achievements for themselves. The limelight must be theirs at all times.

"In their needs, the narce is highly codependent. They depend on the actions of others to make them happy. They do not take responsibility for their own feelings, ever. If they are angry, someone *made* them angry. If they are happy, the actions of someone else *made* them happy. If one does not praise, follow and obey the narce, there are consequences because such people *make* the narce unhappy. Anyone standing up to the narce instantly becomes their enemy."

"That seems so strange to me that merely standing up to a narce causes such rage," I said.

"Yes, it is strange. You see, the narce is fierce in their demands to be obeyed completely. Anyone who does not obey them finds themselves in a difficult position. The narce will not tolerate 'disobedience' and will do all they can to erase a disobedient person from their circle. This type of narce anger is almost always fierce. He or she will actually feel the need to punish and eventually get rid of a perceived enemy. That person, the enemy, won't even know they are the narce's enemy. The narce's anger toward that person will be expressed in aggressive or passive-aggressive ways.

"The narce will often brag up their 'special abilities', but make no mistake! In any group of people, at work or play, the narce may very well be excellent at what they do. They may even be gifted. Superior abilities give the narce no end of pleasure. They will constantly remind everyone that they are the best in the group at this, that, and the other. They will demand constant praise. They thrive on it.

"This craving of theirs never ends. They actually believe that others are obligated to bow out of their way. They also believe that they are entitled to praise, no matter how badly they may treat people. It is accurate to say that they crave adoration, sometimes to the point of being worshiped. This is how true 'cults' may get started, which is another story altogether.

"So, getting back to the narce, either you praise and obey them, or you are their mortal enemy. They believe that you are their enemy simply because you don't think like they do. They want to be the one who mandates how you think and even how you get to feel. Disagree, and you become the enemy."

Frog stopped speaking and watched me carefully. I was scrambling with my notes. Then I stopped writing and looked up. "That seems completely out of the realm of reason, Frog," I said in near disbelief. "I just don't understand."

He studied me for a moment longer. I knew that he truly wanted me to comprehend his teachings. After a moment of contemplation, he continued to speak. "You know, George, this may be hard to understand, but with the narce, there are no other schools of thought *allowed*. There is no acceptable way or means other than that which *they* present. The only time a narce will give into another's ideas is when there are benefits to agreeing."

"Benefits to them agreeing? How?"

"If the group you share with the narce says that your idea is good or better than the narce's, he or she will appear to agree. They choose to capitulate rather than look bad to the group. Understand, though, that the narce will hop on board that bandwagon only until they figure out how to get the limelight back on themselves. They will often try to destroy your credibility and reclaim that attention.

"The narce will ignore all other ideas that they are not pressured to accept by the group. Or, if they can, they will steal the better idea and present it as their own. They will do this without hesitation. The narce can be quite under-handed in business dealings or at work. They will love bomb, earn trust, learn secrets, and then finally take the best ideas of their victim and present them as their own."

"I have seen this happen, before, yes," I said. "But why, Frog? What is the narce's motivation? Money? Power?"

"Well, George, we have already touched on the reason for such behavior: *The narce simply knows in their mind that they are superior to all others. Plus, they believe that their superiority should be obvious to all others.* The narce has this idea that they cannot be one-upped, beaten down, or challenged. They are simply the better person, and that is all there is to it.

"The narce constantly strives to present that superiority and will not hesitate to hurt another to do it. They will make their imagined superiority 'obvious to the group', one way or another. They are willing to get rid of all who disagree or who are better than they are at this or that. That way, their superiority is undisputed."

Frog paused for a moment to let me take in this unbelievable thought. I wrote some things down to catch up. Then he continued when I was up to speed. "You, see, George, the narce is continually competing with 'the other'. 'The other' is *everybody else*. They compete with the rest of the world. The narce keeps a mental and emotional ledger of who has done what in the relationship, whatever type of relationship it is. They will always seek to stay on top, no matter how badly the other person is affected. The competition is brutal and bloody. You may think that the blood is merely figurative, but it can easily become literal, depending on the venue where the competition is taking place.

"The reason for the competition is quite simple: The narce knows himself to be the superior one in all things, times and places. They are legendary in their own minds. What they do is always right at all times, all places, and in all situations. *Whatever they do is right, because they are never wrong.* Let that settle into your mind: *The narce always believes that they are right because they can do no wrong.* In a narce's world, what they are doing must be right because they *cannot* be wrong. They cannot be wrong because they are *superior* to all others. This is black and white, circular, elitist, and illogical reasoning, yes, but the narce carries that into all relationships.

"To the narce, it does not matter how much another suffers. It does not matter how unfair the actions of the narce may be. It does not matter who lives, or who dies. The narce must always come out on top because they are not capable of having things any other way. They cannot stand being in second place, even when no one else is aware of the competition."

"So, Frog, you are telling me that… the narce always believes that there is a winner and a loser. They must win at whatever cost, even if no one else is actually competing."

"Yes, George. Now this part is going to be really hard for you to understand. Where the narce is concerned, forget conscience. Forget empathy for the pain they have caused. They must win the imagined competition at all costs. We will discuss this in depth, later in our lessons."

I was stunned to hear this. I froze for a moment, then asked, "So, they don't care how others react to or are affected by this behavior?" I did know what else to say.

"My friend, they don't care what anyone has to say about it! In their mind, you are wrong to oppose them, no matter what evidence you present to the contrary. In the narce's world, logic and reason do not matter. The narce will overcome your logic and reason by bullying, battering, social destruction, professional humiliation, or any other necessary means. The narce will simply overwhelm you with their words and may even turn your family and friends against you with their clever, underhanded tactics. The rules of fair play, etiquette, and even the right to live one's own life as they see fit do not apply. Those rules are for weaklings not strong enough to dominate others. The narce sees people of conscience and introspection as fodder for them to control by their manipulations."

"But, surely, they must listen to reason," I said in all sincerity.

"You are a good man, George. You don't believe that people like this exist, because it does not seem possible in the normal world. To complete our task, you will need to understand the type of mind you are dealing with.

"To argue with a narce is to waste time. They will never see any way to agree with you. They have no respect for another's opinion. There will be no meeting halfway with any true intent. When a person or group opposes the narce and stands up for their rights, they have a way of dealing with that: The narce uses pleasantry and agreement, which never lasts, as a tool to position themselves to establish or reestablish control over a person or situation.

"The healthy person will see hope for the relationship in the narce's pleasant overtures. In reality, the narce is simply looking for an opening to reestablish control. These phony advances are called 'hoovering', named after a popular household vacuum cleaner. The vacuum metaphor refers to how the narce wants to 'suck' you back into a false sense of security and trust so that they can start the abuse all over again. The victim's belief that the narce has become agreeable gives the narce time to figure out how people think and act. They will watch people closely to find their buttons so they can begin manipulating people."

"This… seems impossible, Frog. It just does."

"Yes, George, I know. I once thought that the scorpion could not possibly sting me halfway across the river and drown us *both*. And yet, that is precisely what he did. So… Tell me… how do my words *feel* to you, George?"

I thought for a moment. Then tears filled my eyes. I shed tears of great sadness, and yet, the words were filled with light. "The words feel true, Frog. I am so sorry to learn all of this, but the words feel true. I have seen some people act this very way. I have been treated this very way. I just did not know why. Knowing that people like this exist is so hard."

"Yes, my friend. It is so hard. I think you have learned enough for one day. Come back tomorrow evening after work. I will be here. We can talk some more."

6

THE FALSE SELF

THE NEXT DAY, after working at my less-than-wholly-satisfying day job, and please never ask me what it was… I took my notes and pens back to Old Man Bryant's pond.

I took my place on the old grist wheel and there was Frog, floating placidly. "Hello, George. How was your day?"

"It went well enough. I could not wait to get back here, though. How was your day, Frog?"

"Well, I ate some insects and did my usual swimming. I held communion with Our Creator. He and I concluded that you should learn about the 'false self.'"

"The false self…? Um… have I done something wrong?"

"You? Oh, heavens, no!" chuckled Frog. "You are very much on track. In fact, I must say that your level of introspection and your sensitive conscience are the two biggest factors that played heavily in the decision to choose you. Your teachability was another weighty factor in our choice. Now, if you would please settle yourself in and prepare to write, I will begin. Ready? Good! Today, you will learn about the 'false self'."

"The false self? Really? What is that?" I asked with great interest.

"The false self is what the narce presents at the beginning of all relationships. It does not matter if it is business, friendly, or romantic. The narce presents themselves as personable, happy, gregarious, and likable. Upon meeting, the narce will always make you think that they really like you.

This is the side of the narce that the world always sees. This is the side of the narce that causes people to believe in them. Others will believe that there is no way the narce could be the problem if you complain against them. When the victim begins to defend themselves to others, many will think the victim is nitpicking. Are you following me, George?"

"I think I understand. I see the narce as gathering their army to bully the victim. The victim does not know what the narce is doing. The narce shows their wonderful, happy side to everyone else as they abuse the victim. Then when the victim stands up for themselves, it is too late. The others already have been poisoned against the victim. They won't believe that the narce is capable of the negative things that the victim reveals. It does not matter that the victim is telling the truth because everyone already believes the narce."

"Precisely," continued Frog. "The overtures of friendship from the narce's False Self draw people in close enough for the narce to choose their friends. These 'friends' are nothing more than tools to use against their victims. The narce finds out what makes potential allies tick. Then the narce manipulates those people to believe that the narce is just wonderful. After the allies are in the narce's corner, they won't believe anything the victim says. Any mutual friends of the narce and victim will usually turn on the victim, with few exceptions.

When the narce wishes to use you as an individual, they become your buddy. The narce is now your pal, and boy, *are they into you*! They want to learn all about you. They make you think they like you, so you trust them. Once they have earned your trust, they can find out what your weaknesses are, what your preferences are, and how they can best use you to suit their personal needs."

"Well, I get that," I interjected. "But the narce cannot keep this charade up all the time. Nobody can stay in character around the clock, can they?"

"No, they can't," continued Frog. "Realize that the false self always is dropped at home, or when the narce is sure that they are alone with the victim. The real self is used on the victim when the narce is comfortable and knows that the victim can't, or won't, fight back. This is a form of control that is exercised by every narce. They become their mean, petty, and spiteful selves to their closest victim, and this leaves the victim confused. They wonder why the narce is two different people. The narce is so kind around others and so mean when they are alone with the victim.

"The victim keeps hoping for a return to the euphoria of the love bombing days that they believed to be the true character of the narce. The victim once felt incredibly loved. Now they are no longer loved. They are now abused. The abuse is very confusing because they 'know' in their heart that the narce loves them."

The light of inspiration suddenly switched on and I said, "So, the victim builds their own prison of false hope. They hold on to the relationship, believing that the 'way it used to be' will come back."

"Precisely, George. Once the narce has the victim squarely in their assigned place, the false self is no longer used on the victim. The victim now sees the narce's true character. The old loving ways return just often enough to keep the victim holding on. While the false self is displayed before the whole world, only the victim knows the truth."

"What does the narce get from this?"

"They get money or other benefits, they look good, they achieve power, and so on. We can lump these perceived advantages under the term 'supply'. We will define and speak more of supply, but later."

"So… we may never really know what they want. We may never know what they gain. But, in any case, they need to come out on top."

"Yes. From the narce's perspective, the world must be, and usually is, convinced that the narce is the good one. When the victim is with the narce and other people are present, the victim is treated well for all to see. The victim plays right along, again holding to the false hope. Plus, the narce is giving them a break from the usual, continual abuse. That break is a welcome respite. When the victim sees the break in the abuse, the false hope that the narce is starting to love them again. But the truth is that the narce never loved them from the beginning. Do you see now?"

"I think so, Frog. That way, the narce can tell the world that their chosen victim is crazy, is wrong, is a liar, and so on when the victim tries to expose the truth. The narce will use their supporters, even as they continue to get manipulate the victim. The narce gets sympathy, support, or some other form of attention. They get an ego boost from the power they hold over the victim, as they watch them writhe around in misery."

"Precisely, my friend. The narce will continue to abuse the victim, who may not accept or even understand that they are being abused. The victims are usually highly empathic people who excuse the narce's actions by thinking 'they are just having a bad day' or 'well, it's just the way they were raised', and so on. Usually, by the time the victim realizes they have been duped if they ever realize this, it has become too late to go to mutual friends for support. It is too late because the friends/family have been taken in by the narce's false self and their social chameleon abilities. It can be very hard now for the victim to try to break free. They will lose much, including family and friends who have been taken in by the narce."

"Aha!" I exclaimed. "So, the narce will only make friends with people who can give them something… and they will use these people to increase their control over the victim, thus gaining power."

"Well said," continued Frog. "Sometimes, the victim comes up from 'under the ether', or in other words, he or she awakens and starts to see through the smoke screen of the false self. Only now, it is very hard to win support. Because of the narce's uncanny ability to fool the masses, the deceived mutual friends and *others will encourage the victim to stay with the* narce. *They will tell the victim that they know that the narce is such a good person.* Their belief in the decency of the narce causes them to unwittingly help him or her continue abusing the victim."

"That is incredible. Narces truly disrespect others to that extreme?" I was shocked and wanted to make sure that I heard right.

"You must remember George, that another person's thoughts, ideas, morals, boundaries, and rights do not matter to the narce. They may agree with the cause of the individual or group up front, but the narce will always make sure that they control everyone, eventually. They will be certain to remove anyone from the group who will not conform to the *narce's ultimate vision*. That vision always ends up with the narce in control. The power the *narce* gets from controlling the group always comes from other people and at their expense. They will not be gentle in their removal, either. They will exercise 'extreme prejudice' in getting rid of the offender."

"Wow," I said, my eyes wide open to new things. "It seems that the narce's entire *modus operandi* depends on keeping everyone in line and trusting their unreal self."

"Yes, George. The false self is created by the narce living as the flawless version of themselves that everyone loves. Everyone who surrounds the narce believes in that false self. The social circle of the narce is always carefully chosen and groomed individually. Each victim, as all people in the narce's circle are victims, is carefully handpicked for what they bring to the group. Once the narce can determine what they want from each victim, they carefully guide them.

Like pieces on a chess board, the narce lines people up, extracts what they want, and then they begin to discard everyone who does not play into their game. Pawns are traded for queens in chess, but in the narces' world, pawns are traded for more useful pawns. The narce always retains the most power. The narce is the queen of the chess board at all times. There are no other queens. The narce's idea is to assign everyone power at their whim, to their own advantage."

"Daaannngg..." I said.

My voice trailed off. I did not know what else to say.

7

NARCISSISTIC BEHAVIOR

FROG PAUSED to allow me time to gather my thoughts. Then, when I stopped writing and looked over at him, he continued. "There are key behaviors that narces display. Once we learn the narce's modes of manipulation, it is easy to pick them out. It is like they all study the same playbook. Whether they are male or female, no matter what race, or national origin, no matter how they self-identify, they all play by the same rules."

"Well, can't people discover these rules and expose the narce?"

"Yes. That is why you are writing this book. You will help people to pick out narcissists. Understand, too, it is *especially* easy for an educated and informed empath to pick out a narce. Only the narce makes the empath feel a certain way. The empath gets this terrible feeling for a moment of what is behind the mask and *poof!* The narce is exposed. I have discovered that once the empath uncovers them, the narce knows it immediately. No words are exchanged; it is simply *known to both parties in the same instant*!

"The narce will immediately turn hateful toward the empath that understands their game. This is because the empath knows the narce's secret. The narce knows that the empath may expose them to the world. Exposure is the one thing the narce does not want above all else. It will ruin the narce's game to have the empath warn the others about him. The narce will not be able to get their manipulative hooks into people who have been warned about his true self.

"The narce does not want anyone to know their true self. Their true self is flawed, and the narce cannot accept those flaws being exposed to the world. If the empath exposes the narce to the world, it is 'game over'. They will lose all of that supply. Losing supply is what the narce fears above all else.

"That narce fear of their real self, George, is why the scorpion stung me. He knew that I could expose him. He knew that he would lose his supply if I ever told anyone the things he did to get a ride out of me. He feared the loss of supply more than death itself. He believed that I would tell everyone of his high opinion of himself. He knew I could expose how powerful he believed himself to be in his community. He knew that the other Scorpions would not approve. He thought that I could not wait to start humiliating him."

I stopped writing. "Well, that was not your intention."

"Of course not. But it was something he *feared*. He was afraid that I would expose him."

I looked perplexed. I did not even quite know what to ask him.

"Ah! You don't quite get the picture. Let me explain… Scorpion and I would have arrived at his home nest at the same time. He would not have the chance to discredit me in the community before I got there. I would have been the center of attention. I would have been the Frog Who Saved the Scorpion. I would have had the spotlight on me. Scorpion could not stand that thought. Not only that, but he believed me to be just like him. He believed that I would expose him to the other Scorpions and cost him his supply. So, in his vanity, he killed us both."

"I… see. It must be terrible to live with that kind of fear."

"It is, and in this case, the Scorpion literally chose suicide over exposure. That is why the narce is so predictable. Their behavior is always the same because they have the same fear. They use the same methods to prevent the realization of that fear because the methods are effective. It is the kindness and empathy in human nature that allow narce's methods to work.

The stages of a narce behavior, which apply to romantic, friendly, business, and all other connections are consistent in every case. These stages are: *Love Bomb, Devalue, Hoover, Discard, Hoover, Discard, Hoover… over and over again until the ultimate discard*. The love bomb traps the victim. The devaluation puts the victim in the place assigned to them. The hoover is used to draw the victim back into their place when the victim is ready to rebel. The ultimate or final discard occurs when the narce is done with the victim. Even after that, they will try to hoover their discarded victim and keep them on the outskirts of their circle 'just in case' they ever need that supply again.

"The narce continues in this pattern, all the while preparing other sources of narcissistic supply to replace the current one. The narce cannot stand to be without supply, so they will be certain that they have other sources out there, ready to go. Remember that they are addicted to supply; they cannot live without it. The more supply in reserve, the better."

"Why do they have so many backups, Frog? Why can't they just keep their providers of supply around them long-term?"

"Well, George, the narce knows that all relationships must end. Whether it is from the narce becoming bored with the victim, or the victim growing weary of abuse, they will inevitably end. The narce must immediately move on to another source of supply. In fact, *the narce already has an expiration expectation for all of their relationships.* They expect the victim to stop playing ball one day. In other words, the narce knows that the victim will likely rebel at some time. They know that with few exceptions victims will not allow the narce to have their way forever.

"As tragic as it is, the narce has to also consider that the physical and/or mental health of the victim may fail, leaving the victim disabled or even *dead*. Not only may the victim die of natural causes, but they may also die prematurely from stress-related illness. Or, tragically, they may commit *suicide*.

"If the victim is the narce's spouse or significant other, then the narce gets a huge supply from the victim's death. They will, by default, become the center of attention. This is especially true if the death is sudden and untimely. Suicide will naturally cause the greatest outpouring of support and all the more supply. The narce will get their way even in the victim's death.

"Commission of suicide by the victim may seem like an extreme response to an abusive relationship, but sometimes the victim cannot see any other way out. Consider the following three points: First, only the victim knows the truth about the narce. Only the victim is harmed by the narce. Even if the victim tells the truth, the narce will discredit the victim. The narce always tries to make sure that no one will believe the victim. There have even been court cases where the judge believed the abusive narce over the victim. This is not for a lack of wisdom, but simply because the narce built such a wonderful case in their own favor. No reasonable person would believe that the narce was at fault after viewing the picture he or she painted of the unreasonable, unstable victim.

"Secondly, the victim suffers greatly at the hands of the abuser. The victim is miserable all of the time. They are constantly browbeaten and sabotaged by the narce. All the while everyone in their circle supports the narce. So, truthfully, the victim has no place to turn. They have no support and they begin to suffer terribly. Their suffering makes it all the harder for them to function. The victim loses their sense of identity.

"And finally, a narce is capable of not only generating false evidence and lying, but they know how to gather others to buy into the lie with them. 'Maybe you did not see it,' says the narce, 'but you believe me, don't you? Well then, just tell the judge and jury that you saw it happen. After all, you know me and you know that I would not lie about such a terrible thing. Without your eyewitness testimony, I will not have a case. You don't want them to get away with this, do you? Could you really live with yourself?'"

The frog paused here to let me gather my thoughts and speak.

"So, people will actually do this? They will perjure themselves on the narce's word only? That's just... I don't even have the words!" I exclaimed, genuinely shocked.

"This is how far the narce will go to control other people to discredit their victim. Remember that the narce is capable of ruining someone without a second thought. Remember that some narces will even kill their victims. So, why would the narce not say whatever they have to say to make the victim look bad? Why would they not use their influence over people to encourage a lie, even in court? Remember that *the things the narce does are always right in their own minds because they can never do wrong.*

"The narce will ruin the victim's reputation by telling people that the victim has this or that weakness. They will make the victim appear incapable, inept, clumsy, and unable to solve problems. The narce will tell everyone that the victim is the source of all the difficulties that they experience. They will even paint the victim as criminally abusive. The narce will even tell mutual friends and family that the victim 'says this' or actually 'thinks that' about them to destroy the trust people place in the victim. There are no limits to what they will do or say to make the victim look bad.

"The narce will always say that they want the victim to succeed, but all the while the narce is sabotaging the victim. They are doing things behind the scenes to block the victim's efforts. The narce does this to keep the spotlight on themselves. They play the victim to everyone around them. *Playing the part of the victim is a huge part of the narce's life, even as they continually work at destroying the actual victim.*"

I paused my writing and looked up. "You mean to tell me, Frog, that the narce will destroy the victim's efforts at success and then actually blame the victim? They will mislead their mutual friends? They will even deceive family and the courts into believing the victim is at fault? They will make people think the victim is *a criminal*? My gosh...!"

"Yes, George, it certainly is terrible. That is why some people get away with such abuse for years and years. The narce has played the part of the delightful character to everyone around them. The narce is kind, funny and such a warm and generous person to everyone else. The narce will completely convert the victim's social circle to their own side if they can.

"The narce taints people's judgment with the 'warm and wonderful person' act to isolate the victim. The victim becomes the only one who knows the truth about the narce. People who once befriended the victim are now in the narce's corner. They believe that they are doing the right thing by siding against the victim.

"This is a surprisingly successful narce tactic. With the narce talking behind them, the victim is not present to defend himself and the narce gets their way with everyone. By the time the victim understands what is actually going on, it is too late for them to win any support. The narce has already won everyone over to their side of the 'argument'. It is possible that the victim did not even know that the narce was so unhappy."

"That is just awful. Why does the narce do such things?" I asked with tears in my eyes.

"The narce has a very 'all or nothing' attitude. In the narce's world, people are not loved to varying degrees, as do normal people. People are 'useful' or 'discarded'. Love does not even enter the equation. The narce's whole social circle has to be under their tight control. Either one is under control and favored or one is not under control and is despised. All people are either a 'yes' or a 'no'. They are either useful or discarded. Everything is absolute and there is no room for compromise. Supply is at the root of all of this."

"Well," I responded, "that seems to be pretty cut and dried. I wonder though, with such an extreme agenda, shouldn't the narce be isolated with only a few followers?"

"That is reasonable to think so, yes, but despite 'all or nothing' the narce can appear to be part of a team. They can appear to be very good team members. They can appear to be very good family members. They can appear to be very kind and agreeable. People respond well to the narce's act because of his charisma. It is interesting to note that every circle out there can be the narce's circle. They can appear to fit into every group.

"They appear to agree with everyone and accept every viewpoint of whatever circle they are in. When they are with churchgoers, the narce is Christian. When they are around the NRA, they are pro-Second Amendment. Then when they are around Muslims, they are open to reading the Koran. When they talk with gun control proponents, they are in favor of stricter gun laws. There can be a collision if opposing groups meet in the presence of the narce at the same time, but this rarely happens because the narce studiously avoids such meetings.

"Even when a social collision does occur, the narce is skilled at wiggling out of awkward situations. They will appear to be "neutral" or "understanding" for the sake of the mixed group but then will reestablish their old positions when alone with the various groups. They will say that they were just trying to avoid conflict in an awkward moment. Ever the peacemaker, you see. We call this the 'chameleon' trait of the narce. They have this uncanny ability to blend in wherever they are, even if they have to change their stance to do it. The narce is ever the social chameleon, always on the offensive and working to manipulate groups."

"But wouldn't changing all the time cause the narce to lose control of their victims? Can't the victim capitalize on the chaos and show the world what is wrong?" I asked.

"Actually, it is to the contrary. The narce thrives on chaos, even as it exhausts the victim. Chaos keeps the victim off balance and confused. This causes drama because the victim will eventually question the narce about all the nuttiness. The victim does not understand why the narce must deceive and undermine people. The excitement of the confusion, chaos, and drama keeps the narce going. The control they exert over others and the power of the confusion they create is a significant source of narce supply. Not only that, but if the victim does come forward and tries to discredit the narce, it won't work. People will believe and side with the narce who says that the victim has something against him or her, or is trying to cover up their own faults somehow by smearing at them. This is surprisingly effective, even in the face of bold evidence to the contrary. If the victim tries to expose him, the narce will claim that the victim is just gossiping and trying to cause trouble.

"Narces also thrive on the suffering that they cause in the victim. The victim will eventually receive injury from the narce's insane lifestyle. The more it hurts the victim, the more the narce does it. To the narce, the victim deserves the punishment they are receiving. Everyone who disagrees with the narce, as the victim often does, is flat wrong. Because they are wrong, they deserve to be punished."

"That seems so irrational and terrible."

"That is because you are a reasonable, kind, and thoughtful person. Such people cannot think the way the narce does. It does not seem possible that anyone would want such a life. But remember that the narce *thrives on drama.* They don't care what happens to others when they are trying to get their way. They use chaos to keep their victims off balance. It is a useful tool because it is a great source of narce supply."

"Wow… again… This is so… crazy," I mused out loud.

"To mix drama with the chaos, the narce will constantly pick fights where there should be none. When they engage the victim in an argument is an exercise in verbal jousting that continually runs in circles and goes nowhere. There is no winning of such arguments. The narce simply dismisses the victim's logic and reason until the victim is worn out by the conflict."

"So, the narce is skilled at manipulating words. Does the victim ever win?" I asked earnestly.

"The narce will never let the victim win the argument, unless there is a reason that benefits the narce. For instance, the narce might let the victim win to allow the victim to think they are making some headway. This is one of the many types of false hope that the narce loves to use. It keeps the victim hopeful for the relationship. Otherwise, the arguments have no logic, make no sense, and keep going on and on until the victim just surrenders out of exhaustion.

"During these arguments, or 'conversations' as the narce will call them, they constantly pick apart the victim by criticism. It is important to remember there is nothing sacred to the narce. There are no boundaries they will not cross. In fact, to the narce, the victim has no boundaries. The narce is without empathy and they actually enjoy causing the victim to feel terrible about themselves. The worse they feel about themselves, the weaker they are. The weaker the victim is, the stronger the narce feels!

"The only important thing to the narce is their perceived advantages. The narce will never accept defeat. They will always believe themselves to be on top, no matter what. They are not capable of believing anything else. I believe this is because someone or some situation in life taught them that being the 'winner' is all that matters. To be on top is the only way to be. The narce does not care who or what they must destroy to get whatever it is they want."

"Now, come on, Frog!" I spoke with a touch of irritation. "There cannot be anyone out there like that."

"Well, George..." started Frog patiently and carefully. "Understand where I am coming from. I have lived for hundreds and hundreds of years. I have seen kings and dictators come and go. I have seen the narcissistic need for supply fulfilled in the most unimaginably perverse and violent ways. It is never easy for a man of your personality type to believe that such people exist. But think... what about the well-known tyrants in human history? Stalin, Hitler, Mussolini, Vlad the Impaler... What about them?"

"Yes, but these were powerful dictators!"

"Indeed. But... think of this... did they start so powerful? Or were they born as helpless babes?"

"They were born helpless, of course..." my voice trailed off thoughtfully.

"Yes. And then they gathered a following, using what?"

"The ability to convince people that they were right and deserved—Oh!"

"'Oh', what, George?"

"These dictators started with small followings who thought they had good ideas..."

"Yes. Then?"

"Then the narce's groups became larger. The narce then started socially abusing groups. The narce began to blame the victims of their abuse for society's ills. They made speeches to their followers, saying that the victims deserved what they got. They would lie to the crowd about the victims… Oh, my…"

My head slumped forward. I could not believe what I just learned. After I shook my head for a moment, I continued with, "Narces are just dictators on a small scale. They may not have as much power as Stalin, Hitler or other dictators of the world, but I suddenly realize that they have the same *attitude*.

"The only reason that smaller-scale narces don't do what the bigger boys and girls do is that they don't have the power of armies and navies to back them up! On their smaller scale and in their own circle, the narces from among the average ranks use the same tactics as the most horrific tyrants in human history!" I was still stunned at my realization. I just sat there, dumbfounded. I did not move. I simply stared into space for a moment.

"George?" asked frog. "George, my boy… are you okay?"

"But… the most terrible tyrants were mass murderers."

"Yes, George, they were. The vast majority of narces don't become mass murderers or kill even a single person. But you are right. These 'smaller' narces do follow in the footsteps of the great tyrants' methods, nonetheless. Keep in mind, too, *that even though a narce may not 'kill' anyone, they* do *destroy lives and happiness.* 'Character assassination' is called that for a reason. You may ruin a life without actually taking it. Ruining someone can be about as terrible as killing them."

I was completely astonished and quiet for a few minutes while taking this all in. I could not believe it. *I realized that the narces of the world are no different than the warmongers who commit genocide. They are no different than tyrannical kings and queens. They are just smaller and less powerful. Even though only a small percentage of narces become killers, the inner workings are much the same.* I closed my eyes and just sat there, pondering over the situation.

Finally, I opened my eyes again. I looked down and Frog was sitting on my leg, looking up at with me concern. "Yes, Frog, I am okay now. Thanks for your concern. If you are more comfortable back in the water, you may go. I appreciate you hopping up here to sit on my leg. That was actually a comfort, old friend. Thank you. Now… back in the water… there you go. You looked like you were drying out. I am feeling much better now. Thank you. So, getting back to the matter at hand… What possible goal does the narce have in mind?"

"Well, George, that's an excellent question. What would any narce want if they were simply tyrants on a smaller scale? They all want *dominance*. The narce's goal is to get the victim to agree to the narce's terms of the relationship. Or, if the victim refuses the terms, then the narce wishes to leave the victim ruined and completely alone. That is why it is so important for the narce to get to the social circle of the victim.

"If the victim obeys the narce's every whim, the only win the victim gets is the opportunity to remain in the narce's good graces… temporarily. The relationship will only last long enough for the narce to get all the supplies they can from the victim. Once the supply runs out, the narce will casually and coldly discard the victim. At the discard, the victim will end up hurt, frustrated, and potentially alone. It will not matter how hard they worked to please the narce."

"That's… that's *terrible*!" I exclaimed.

"Indeed, it is, George. The narce loves to create circumstances that cannot be solved and then blames the victim. The narce may do something like get into a relationship and buy a house together with the victim. Things will seem fine, but once the narce gets the home they wanted, they will quit their job or spend all the money, or do both. The victim will be left to make a house payment they cannot afford. Then the narce will blame the victim when they miss the house payments and finally lose the home.

"This lose and blame, lose and blame scenario will just happen over and over again. Houses, cars, apartment leases… you name it. The narce will demand things, set things up so they can afford them, then take all the money meant for the bill and blow it. Meanwhile, the whole time, the narce denounces the victim as they present to the world that the loss is all the victim's fault.

"People will start to see the victim as inept when they are not. The truth is that the victim is being intentionally and coldly sabotaged. The narce wants the victim to look bad, even if they must intentionally do things to hurt them *both. This is what I like call the 'Scorpion Effect'*, referring, of course, to my experience with my 'friend', Scorpion, who drowned us both.

"That being said, during their various acts of sabotage, the narce will not hesitate to gang up on the victim. They do this by using the network they have built up among their common circle of family and friends, as we have already discussed.

"Speaking of 'ganging up'… while family and friends are the most accessible, strangers are also useful. With strangers, the narce has fresh and clean slates upon which to fabricate the life they had with the victim. The total strangers who are being love-bombed will often believe the narce and side with them, as well. They may even throw in with the narce and help them damage the victim further. They are usually good people who think they are doing a good thing.

"This works so well because the narce will tell a stranger all kinds of intimate details of the relationship. They will paint themselves in glowing terms while destroying the victim's reputation. If the victim walked into a room full of the narce's new compatriots, they would feel contempt in the room. Any attempt to defend themselves would be met with caustic disbelief. The victim has already lost without even a chance to defend themselves.

"One more thing that narces all will do without exception: *they will hate, with venomous stings, anyone who refuses to play their game.* They will not only snub the victim, but *they will also snub and try to ruin anyone who is on the victim's side.* This is because the narce has to have everyone in their circle on their side. Anyone who does not play by the narce's rules will be discredited. The narce discredits them because of their fear of exposure.

"The narce lives a lie and if the truth is ever known, that will end the narce's influence over people. To the narce, losing power is the end of life itself. The narce feels entitled to all things they desire, no matter what the cost. From wealth to the pettiest emotional needs, they believe they are entitled to all they desire and there is no changing their mind. This is not, of course, how the world works. This is merely the narce's perception. They create their world and their circle that supports that belief."

"Wow…" I could say nothing else. After writing notes and impressions on all of that, I noticed the time. The bugs were coming out and lighting on the water. Frog needed to make his living. Besides, my brain was full and I had a lot to process. I suggested we end our lesson, and Frog agreed.

Before hopping out to catch his dinner, he advised me to take a couple of days off, to let all of this settle into my mind comfortably. I agreed completely. I was actually having a very difficult and sorrowful time with my new understanding.

We bade our good nights and I slowly wandered home to settle into a fitful night's sleep. My difficulty sleeping was rooted in the realization that people are capable of being so rotten to others. I understood, like most people, that criminals, kings, and rulers can be very selfish. That was just sort of a given that we read about every day as we grew up.

However, I had never considered that common individuals could be so willing to force their ways onto others. I had never before contemplated the idea that people are capable of "tyranny" in their personal relationships to the degree of destroying lives. I used to think that power was the sole source of corruption in people. I did not realize that people could already be corrupted first and *then* seek power. I wondered, too, if narces are born or made…

8

HOW THE VICTIM BEHAVES

I APPEARED at the pond a couple of days later. I believe it was a Saturday. The weather was pleasant and I was able to digest what Frog had taught me during our latest lesson. I realized that, yes, I had seen narc abuse many times and places. It showed up in the cases of a schoolyard bully, an abusive spouse, a mean significant other, an overbearing boss, a misguided clergyman, or an egotistical doctor. Narces are everywhere! I had also come to the tough realization about the victim: *Instead of recognizing the abuse, victims often believe that they failed in the relationship.*

I found Frog sitting on the millstone this time. I guess I had never before considered that a frog could have facial expressions. It surprised me that he appeared *concerned*.

"George!" he called. "Are you doing okay today?"

"Yes, Frog. I am doing okay," I smiled. "Why do you appear so concerned?"

"Well, when you left the other day, I felt that you might not come back. Are you here to work, or are you here to tell me you can't continue?"

"I am here to work, Frog," I said resolutely as I showed him my pad and pens. "I had considered quitting, yes. I went home and thought things over. I began to realize that we have narce abuse all over the place. We have it in homes, hospitals, clubs, churches, the workplace… you name it.

"In fact, while at my day job, I began to realize that I was seeing narce behavior at the office. We have this one boss in particular, who uses anger to control his subordinates. He yells and curses at anyone beneath him, but is sweet as honey around the other bosses or people he wants to influence. Then, once he gets you under his influence, he becomes the opposite of how he presented himself… He gets what he wants out of you, then abuses you. None of us like working for him. Even some of the other bosses no longer trust him. Love bombing, devaluing, hoovering, and even discards… I see now how it works in real life.

"Not only that, but I have had several failed relationships. I thought the failures were entirely my fault. Now I understand that these relationships were doomed to fail. Failure was built into them by narce abuse. Granted, I am not perfect, so I believed my imperfections alone destroyed the relationship. I think differently now, understanding how narce abuse works."

"Well, George," said Frog, "we knew what you had been through and that was another factor we considered before selecting you. I am happy that you will continue this project with me. I have had other writers working with me who quit right about at this point of their realizing the truth."

"It got too hard for them to see the reality. They could not believe it," I supposed aloud.

"Yes," said Frog. "Their sensitivities were offended, painfully offended, and they thought that maybe I was deceiving them. A couple of them could not accept that they were victims in current narce relationships. One felt so offended at the truth that she said I was a demon of some kind and tried to rebuke me in the name of Our Creator."

"How did that go?" I smiled.

"I just sat there in the water and quietly stared at her. When I did not disappear in hellfire and green smoke, she was surprised. I just continued staring and croaking at her like a frog. Then, she just scoffed and walked away. I guess she felt that she had exorcised a frog and went home. Who knows what she did with her notes?"

"Aren't you afraid that she will tell someone?"

"George, *who is she going to tell?* And tell them what? That she was taking dictation from an ageless frog? They would lock her up."

"I guess so," I said thoughtfully. "There really is no way for her to keep credibility."

"Nope."

"Since you want this story told, I will have to do it as a metaphorical work. That way, people will not think that I am completely unhinged."

"Exactly. Now… Let's get going on this."

I settled onto the millstone and Frog hopped back into the water. He seemed to be gathering his thoughts. I waited patiently until he finally began to speak.

"You finally have accepted that narces really do exist in real life. Now you understand we actually have people in this world who are tyrants in their everyday lives. Now you see the importance of this work… are you ready to continue?"

"Yes." I readied my pen.

"Today, we will take a closer look at the narce's victims, how they are selected, and how they behave. It is all done intentionally and very carefully. Remember that the narce does not like 'accidents' and has a real need to control people. They will always choose people pleasers who have a desire to help or serve the narce. They will pick people who will try to please him in any way the narce demands. Such pliability is necessary for the narce's purposes. The victim will often be required to change their social and family circle to one that pleases the narce.

"Even during abuse, the victim will often apologize for and justify the narce's behavior. This enables the narce to continue abusing them. The victim likely believes that they *caused* the abuse. The narce will always tell the victim something like, 'You are with me for a reason. I know you better than you know yourself and I can help you with your troubles.' To put up with such talk, the victim likely has a poor self-image and little belief in themselves. The victim will believe that the narce has their best interests at heart. When they are inescapably abused, the victim will think that if they were to 'improve', then the abuse would stop.

"However, this is not to say that all who fall for a narce are people of little achievement or low self-esteem. The love bombing stage of the narce relationship can cause great euphoria in the intended victim. The narce may take a different route with people who have self-esteem and strong self-images. Such will not take abuse or easily become a victim. Narces will earn the trust of strong people and use them as leaders in their cause. These leaders are victims of a sort, but they are not the type of people who will tolerate abuse. Remember that the narce does not care how they take power; they just care that power is theirs."

"What if the narce cannot earn the trust of the strong?"

"The narce will simply discard them. Narces will not mess with people they cannot control. We have already discussed how relationships are never permanent in the narce's mind. Remember that the narce is always love bombing, devaluing, and discarding people. The love bomb stage is long enough to get the victim hooked. Then the devaluing will occur to the tolerance of the individual in question. The discard is always in the narce's mind. It will always happen when the narce becomes bored or knows that the person in question will no longer provide them with supply. The discard is not personal, no matter how personal it may seem. The discard is strictly *business;* the business of the narce is to take power over others.

"In many narce abuse cases, the victim will develop a type of Stockholm's Syndrome, accepting any crumb of kindness the narce throws to them as a sign of hope. This is what we refer to as 'bread crumbs' in the narce relationship. The bread crumbs are kind acts from the narce that give the victim hope of keeping the relationship alive. Bread crumbs are given when the victim is preparing to end the relationship or is not as committed to the relationship as the narce would like. The bread crumbs are given not out of regret or kindness, but out of necessity.

"Sometimes, the narce just wants to toy with the individual, controlling them and making them acquiesce to their will. It could really be just that simple. The narce may simply enjoy having a person do certain things on occasion. Again, only the narce knows what they are getting out of the relationship. The only thing we can all be sure of is that the narce has some kind of control over the victim, who submits to the narce every time.

"The victim will often believe that they are dealing with a person of normal conscience and empathy. So, they will do anything they must to keep the relationship alive. They will do so out of sincerity and an interest in the narce's feelings. They want to help the narce to actually achieve what we call a *fake future*, not knowing that this beautiful picture is purely a fabrication.

"A 'fake future' is a series of goals for the relationship that the narce just made up to give the victim a desirable vision. The victim believes in the relationship and the narce, so it makes sense to believe in their future together. The narce uses this to cement the relationship by creating a future that will appeal to the victim. Whatever the victim wants most, the narce will climb aboard that grand vision. It does not matter to the narce how simple or elaborate the dream is, because they have no intention to help build it. All that matters to the narce is that they are in control of their victim.

"The victim may see the evidence presented before their very eyes that the narce is not interested in the fake future, but they won't believe it. To the victim, their intuition must be wrong. The narce 'cannot be serious' or 'must be upset' when they say outrageous things to the victim such as 'Love does not matter, really' or 'Your paycheck means more to me than anything else'. The victim will strive for the fake future because they believe that they will have it. They believe that the narce wants it.

"To try and realize the fake future, the victim will modify themselves in all sorts of ways to reduce conflict, to make the relationship work. The narce will embrace and then consume the changes that the victim makes. The narce will always use the victim's flexibility to their own advantage. They will give the victim false hope that their efforts will make it all better. Then the narce will turn around and say that the changes were not enough.

The victim will then 'try harder' without realizing that anything they do will never be enough. The changes the victim makes will become so obvious that friends and family will no longer recognize the victim. This is because the victim will give up any things that make themselves happy. They will change to please the narce. The victim will often take on a new, reduced, and diminished identity based on the narce's pleasure. They become a shell of what they used to be.

"The narce will know their victim very well. They will be able to predict how the victim will react to stimuli. They will continually provoke the victim into defending themselves by pushing their hot buttons. This will cause a mere disagreement to escalate to a full-blown argument. The narce does all of this intentionally and with great relish.

"The whole purpose for the button-pushing, intentional escalation is to create an excuse to say to the victim 'See how unreasonable you are?' The narce will also rush to tell others what happened and will claim it is the victim's unreasonable behavior that caused the fight. If the narce can make this happen in front of other people, including their children, then so much the better.

"The trouble is that this behavior creates a very effective trap. The victim falls for this narce trap every time because the narce knows how to irritate the victim. They push them to the point of provocation. The narce is very well practiced at this.

"In some cases, the victim will mirror the narce's behavior. This means to use the narce's behavior against them. The victim may do this to show the narce how unreasonable and painful their behavior is. The victim is trying to effect changes in the narce by appealing to their better nature. This is doomed to fail because the narce does not see any reason to change in the first place. They won't change because they know they are always right.

"Meanwhile, the victim may be able to mirror the narce's negativity for a little while, but now the narce has dragged the victim into some 'pig wrestling'. The narc is well-practiced at this kind of negative fighting. This form of arguing is not going to improve relations between the narc and the victim. These arguments are simply a source of amusement and supply for the narc.

"The victim cannot outwit the narc in new, strange territory because the victim is not willing to take the extreme steps necessary to win. The victim is not willing to say the terrible things necessary to overwhelm the narc. The victim is not willing to lie, to use half-truths, and to contradict themselves. They are not willing to deny things that they have previously said. In other words, *the victim is lousy at narc behavior.*

"Mirroring is a terrible idea because when the victim mirrors narc behavior, they have just performed abuses against the narc. The victim has just done something out of character. In so doing, they have entered a dark place. The darkness is usually not familiar territory to the victim, particularly if they are an empath. They have just entered the pigsty of the narcissist and if they are not careful, they can be caught up in a 'tit for tat' game that is very danger-ous. They could get caught up in a game of revenge and lose themselves entirely.

"Not only that, but the narc has just trapped them. The narc now has more tools to use against the victim. Remember that in these relationships, the victim, being normal and mature, wants to work things out privately, as it should be. Therefore, the victim remains quiet, not wishing to bring the world into their problems.

"The narc is exactly the opposite. They make the victim's negative, mirrored behavior known to as many people as possible. They use this as a weapon against the victim. People will think that the victim has something wrong with them. The behavior that the narc describes to everyone is way out of character for the victim. They would have never guessed that the victim was capable of such things. The narc will present to the group that they are 'just trying to help' the victim. The narc, indeed has become an actual victim of abuse… even though it was intentionally engineered.

"With all of this going on, the narce now has all the more supply. For the rest of their lives the narce can tell the victim 'Well, I still remember that time when…' The narce may also say 'If I am so wrong, then why did you do the very same thing back to me?' The victim will not have a leg to stand on. They will have no defense against the narce's rationalization because the narce is right… *the victim did commit the act(s) of abuse.* The narce will show zero tolerance or understanding. And there will be no forgiveness. The victim has just given the narce more power.

"Again, the victim does not understand that the narce is serious about the terrible things they say. The victim will try to continue to deal with the narce, treating the narce a normal person. The victim will not realize how much they are being manipulated as they do so. They will not realize that they are being manipulated because they do not yet realize how cruel and cunning the narce is. The victim, depending on life experience, may not even realize that they are being abused.

"A normal person would try to work their way through the argument or problem by using rationale, logic, forgiveness, give-and-take reasoning, and so on. The narce does not need these things unless they can gain some sort of supply by putting on a show. The victim will not understand yet that narces play by different rules than normal people.

"Because the narce is so cunning and can blame their behavior on the victim, it will cause the victim to feel awful. The victim will then start and continue to blame themselves for any failure in the relationship, based on the mirrored behavior that the narce will not forget or forgive.

"The victim will self-blame because they will see themselves in a *new darkness*. The narce will convince the victim that any failure in their relationship and life, generally is the victim's fault because of the darkness that is in the victim. In likelihood, that 'darkness' is nowhere near the degree of the narce's own dark soul. The narce will speak and act without mercy as they hold 'conversations' with the victim about this darkness. These conversations are nothing more than mental and emotional bullying and blaming.

"The narce will never take any responsibility for the troubles they have and will continue to blame the victim for the very misery the narce generates. The victim will then start to fall for any breadcrumb of hope that the narce leaves for the relationship. The victim may even continue to be the victim for many years and not realize that are being played and manipulated." Frog paused and looked at me. He seemed to expect a response. I finished writing my final thought.

I looked at him and asked, "Why does the victim not simply rebel against the narce?"

"Ah... the golden question. You are praying the answer is simple. Well, your prayer is answered. The victim simply does not have the heart to cut off the relationship. You see, the narce will only choose a target that is loving and kind enough to think only the best of others. The narce sees normal empathy for others as 'weakness'. In a way, the narce is correct because the victim will love the narce and stay with them no matter how terrible the abuse becomes. This is called a 'trauma bond'. The victim will stay bound by that bond until they gather enough education and strength to break free.

"Understand that there is more to breaking free than simply leaving. The victim may have gained enough light and hope to leave the narce, but they will *not* learn to break free of the trauma bond for quite some time. The sad thing is that some light-filled, loving, and empathic people will not ever recover from the trauma bond without help and education. If they don't get some kind of counseling, they will potentially live the rest of their lives believing themselves to be a failure.

"Remember we talked about how narce victims commit suicide? Some of those do it on the misguided notion that the narce and others will see how sorry the victim was for 'ruining the life' of the narce. The fact of the matter is that the narce is the one who ruined the victim's life. We already spoke of how the true narce will use even the death of the victim to their advantage."

"That... is terribly sad..." I said. Even the very thought of the victim taking their own life pained me. This was especially so in light of my new under-standing. I had learned from Frog that the narce would only use that victim's suicide for more supply. The narce would actually see the victim's death as a victory for themselves. In the narce's distorted reality, the victim's suicide would prove that the narce was stronger than the victim, that he was right all along.

I reasoned out on my own that the narce would see the suicide as a result of the victim's self-loathing. The narce would believe that they were better and mightier than the victim and that the victim was pathetic. In the narce's mind, "might make right" and the victim's "weakness" makes them all wrong.

In the end, the narce would not learn anything from the suicide at all. Outside of getting supplies, the victim's suicide would mean little to nothing to the narce. They would not learn that change is needed; they would simply move on to their new supply. "Another weakling bites the dust" would be their credo.

9

NARCISSISTIC THINKING

"Yes," said Frog. "It is terribly sad. I can see in your eyes that you now understand how the narce would use suicide for their own gain and benefit. They would use it as a source of new supply. You are correct. I had a different topic in mind to discuss, but this is a perfect segue into how a narce thinks. We have touched on this, yes, but now we are going into it a little deeper.

"The narce believes that whatever things they think are always and infallibly correct, no matter who, what, where, when, why or how. So, what if the thoughts the narce has are untrue? Well, *their thinking is so flawed that most of their thoughts, conclusions, and beliefs are untrue.*

"Understand that the narce can be right about many things. They can excel in their career. They can be very smart. They can be very capable. They can be very powerful and highly praised. They can achieve. Success is often not a problem for the narce. The problem for the narce, though, is *the truth about who they are and the truth about right vs. wrong.*

"The truth about themselves is a perpetual enemy to the narce. Because the narce cannot stand the truth, they will do everything they can to block facing it. They have no real ability to perform a 'checkup from the neck up'. They have no way to examine their mind and heart because that is too painful for the narce. The narce will not be introspective or soul search. That is because the narce is always right; they must be because they are never wrong. Not only that, but the ends justify the means. To think otherwise is too painful.

"Ultimately, nothing is good enough for the narce. They may have periodic happiness or perhaps a little satisfaction, but it never lasts. The narce sets their goal on things outside of themselves. If they want money, $10 Million makes them happy for a moment, but soon needs to be $20 Million, $20 Million must become $30 Million, and so on. If they want attention, then five friends must become ten, ten to fifteen, and so on. The narce is always goal-oriented and looking for ways to fill their coffer with whatever they need at the time. Once the 'need' is filled, they discover that they have not found happiness or contentment, so they move on to get more supply.

Because the narce is so centered on what they want at the moment, complete and total ingratitude is the rule of the day. The narce has an attitude of entitlement and the victim must comply. The narce thinks the victim must provide for all of their demands, or the narce will punish them continually until the final discard. The narce's attitude, no matter how much supply they have received, no matter how ragged the victim has become from their life together, will always be one of 'Yeah, but what have you done for me *lately*?'

"One of the hardest lessons for the victim to learn is that they were but a tool in the narce's tool box. The victim was nothing more than an object to be used and discarded at will. But, the victim should always be there no matter what. The narce believes that all people are there to serve them. When someone refuses, then the narce will discard that person as easily as they would discard an old, rotten shoe.

"As far as the narce is concerned, the sandbox (our world) is theirs and they get to decide 'who is froze and goes.' There is no second-guessing the narce; they are always in control of the people around them. Anyone who will not be controlled by the narce will be discarded. The narce cannot tolerate anyone whom they cannot control. The narce has no conscience or any type of barometer that will allow them to gauge right and wrong with any accuracy. *The narce is always right... period.*

"The narce has no sense of boundaries, either. Everyone in the *narce's* circle has very few, if any, secrets. The narce knows the weaknesses and flaws of their victim. The narce convinces the victim to share their life with him or her. The victim shares these things out of trust. But he or she does not return the favor because if the narce reveals weaknesses, then they are vulnerable. He must always appear strong and superior to their victim. The *narce* must not appear vulnerable if they are to stay in control and collect their supply.

"It is important to know and understand that the narce does not need a confession from the victim to discover a weakness. The narce is very good at reading body language. They can discover secrets by reading a flicker of an eyelid. The smallest changes of the corners of the mouth, the flaring of the nostrils, a glance in any direction is very telling to a practiced narcissist. They have learned from a young age to 'read' people's expressions and body language to detect any weakness so they may control their victim.

"You see, the desperate need for control is rooted in a core narce belief. *The narce believes that the rest of the world is as vicious and underhanded as they are.* They project their whole personality onto the rest of the world. If the narce is a greedy opportunist, then the rest of the world must be greedy opportunists. If the narce is out to take social advantage, then the rest of the world must be out to take social advantage. The narce will never believe in anyone else's virtues. The narce believes that everyone's virtues are as false as their own.

"Truth is relative to the narce; what they say is true simply because they are the ones saying it. What they believe is true must be true because they are the ones believing it. Logic and facts do not mean anything at all to the narce. Don't bother to try and convince them they are wrong. You, whoever you are, just don't matter. *Only narce is right, only the narce thinks correctly, only the narce knows the one true way.* They cannot believe anything else because the thought that they might be wrong is just too painful for them to bear.

"In fact, narces are in so much pain that they cannot live with themselves. They may show the world a semblance of kindness, but beneath that kindness is a terrible pain. Even the smallest exposure to that pain will cause the narce to lash out. This is why the narce sets such tight boundaries for themselves and works so hard to hide their true selves. Their true self is imperfect and flawed. They cannot stand the idea of being less than perfect, so they hide their imperfections and punish anyone who gets close enough to see those flaws.

"To hide their imperfections, the narce creates boundaries where no one may cross. The narce is not going to share themselves. They are not going to show their underbelly of weakness. They will only share their false selves and will make the world think they are sincere.

"On the other hand, the narce thinks the victim is not allowed to have boundaries at all. Victims are beneath them and they must know where the victim is, what they are doing, what they eat, and most importantly of all… *how the victim thinks and feels*. They want to be in control of the entire person. They want the person whole. The narce must bend people to their will. That is what their behavior is all about.

"It is childish, irrational, and amoral, but it is the narce's way. The victim will be the kind of person who wants to help and will sacrifice themselves to try and help the narce. The narce knows this and that knowledge will keep them in the driver's seat."

"So, the narce makes everyone around them subservient?"

"Yes."

"And the narce likes it?"

"Not just 'like', George. They *live* for it. The narce believes that subjugating all people around them gives them life and power. The fact is, though, the more they succeed at controlling people, the colder and darker they become. This cycle continues until the victim can no longer stand the narce, but they will remain because they fear the narce. The narce will usually have some advantage in the victim's life that the victim cannot loosen. It could be a financial or material, spiritual, legal, emotional, or social/family condition that keeps the victim in a stranglehold.

"Think for a moment of Adolph Hitler's last days. Even his top generals did not dare to give him bad news. Hitler did not tolerate bad news because he needed so very badly to be right. By the time his top brass had no choice but to reveal how badly the Nazi war effort was going, well, it was too late. The Third Reich fell, despite people's loyalty to *der führer*. The narcissism of Hitler, the very drive that caused him to try to rule the world, was the same drive that destroyed his ambitions.

"In the end, instead of facing the consequences of his failure, Hitler took his own life. He may have lost control of everything else, but he did have control over his decision of where and when to die. He was that determined to stay in control. He even dragged his lover into that pit with him, after marrying her. They committed suicide together. That, George, is one of the most graphic examples of the sad, destructive cycle of the narce and the victim."

"*Phew!* That… really troubles me. I mean, yes, I know it is true. But it hurts to know that people have not learned from such examples. The worst of it is that the narce may not be capable of learning."

"Yes. That is the worst part of it. Go home and organize your notes. Then rest a little. Get your mind off the darkness because if you don't, it can wear you out. I will see you tomorrow if you feel like you are ready for more."

1 0

THE IMMEDIATE SOCIAL EFFECTS OF NARCE ABUSE

FROG and I resumed our talk the next day. I was doing okay, able to process what we learned. Frog continued his instruction after checking me over. He asked me a couple of questions about how I slept and ate. Only then did he resume teaching me.

"To say one *survives* narce abuse is not overdramatizing because people lose their health, sanity, and lives over narcissistic abuse. One of the first things that the narce will do is to convince the victim that they have their best interests at heart. They do this even as they build themselves up on the victim's labors. Today, we will go deeper into the social abuses we have already discussed in part.

"The narce will spend the victim's money, take up the victim's time and get rid of anyone in their victim's life who loves and supports them. They get rid of people because those in the victim's life who love them will give them a support system. Outside support will take the victim out from under narce control. The narce cannot have that. The victim is a tool for their use. No one else must be allowed to encourage the victim to stand against being used.

"The narce truly believes that they are smarter, better, and more deserving than the victim. They spend all of their time thinking of ways to use the victim to keep their false self in place. The narce will not hesitate to tell everyone the victim is a fool and will use tactics of control to keep the victim in their 'assigned' role.

"The narce will be so repetitive in their message that the victim will soon believe that they need the narce in their life. They will become convinced that the narce is their only hope. All the while, the narce continuously sabotages the victim. The narce allows the victim to have some success, but when great successes are within the victim's grasp, the narce takes them away. The narce actually gets supply from taunting the victim with hopes of success only to watch the narce torpedo those successes.

"The narce will make sure that the victim's book is never written. If it's written, the narce will torpedo publication and sales. They will make sure that the victim fails at the job where they have just been promoted, by withdrawing needed support, or by creating obstacles. The narce will secretly blast the reputation of the victim behind their back to make sure that golden, deserved opportunities will never come the victim's way. In a nutshell, the narce will go out of the way to destroy the victim's opportunities. Then they will taunt the victim for not succeeding.

"The narce abuser takes advantage of weakness and plays the victim's emotions like a finely tuned violin. They use the victim's feelings against them. The music from the violin is as beautiful or as ugly as the narcissist makes it. The narce is so good at it that the victim does not even know they are being *manipulated.*

"The narce may speak encouraging words to the victim's friends while the victim is present. They will later change the tune when the victim is not around. It would start with something like: 'Now that they are gone, let me tell you what is *really happening around our place…* '"

"That sounds perfectly awful," I said. "That is terrible and hard to believe, but in the light of what I have been learning from you about narces and their lack of respect and failure to recognize boundaries, that seems to all add up."

"It may seem too terrible to believe, but this is precisely what the narce does with the victim. The victim will think things are fine and that the narce supports their dreams and hopes, but nothing can be further from the truth. *The narce will always sabotage the victim*, even when it makes suffering for both of them. Then when the narce starts suffering they will turn to family and friends and showcase that suffering.

"Narces must be the center of attention. They love playing to the crowd. The narce will even turn their mutual children against the victim. They do so by earning the trust of the children. The narce will do nice things for the kids, maybe even secretly, to make them the 'favorite parent', the 'fun' one."

"I see. Because of the narce's kind façade, the victim does not know that the damage is intentional. They don't understand that the narce plans to purposefully sabotage them. The children will keep the secret of the narce parent to keep having fun. The friends and family will keep secrets of the narce because they believe the victim is a bad one."

"Yes. The narce keeps many secrets from the victim. The fact is that the victim really does not know who the narce is because of the false self and the many masks the narce wears. They have no idea that the 'real' narce is doing all that harm."

"So, narces thrive on attention and harming the victim without revealing their true self."

"Yes. And not only is there the attention factor, but the narce gets a thrill out of the harm they cause. Sabotage confuses the mind of the victim. The poor victim cannot understand why things are not working. No matter how much they try, they cannot succeed. The narce criticizes the victim for the very failures the narce causes, and this makes the victim suffer from self-doubt.

"While the narce may say to the victim's face that they want them to succeed, this is really the last thing the narce wants. *The* narce *is afraid of the victim's success. They are afraid that people will start to see how great the victim is at this or that and support them. This takes the spotlight off of the* narce. The narce cannot have that because he or she must be at the center of attention.

"Note that this narcissistic view of the victim's success is completely wrong. The victim, likely an empath, would gladly share the spotlight with the narce.

The narce is too shortsighted, though, to understand that. Even if they did understand that the empath would share, the narce would be too selfish to share. The spotlight must be theirs and theirs alone.

"Now, there is only one form of success that the narce will not sabotage. That is the success that the victim creates under the narce's direction. If the victim will become what the narce tells them to become, that is fine. Why? Well, because then the narce can take credit for the victim's success. They can tell everyone that the victim succeeded only because the narce told them how to succeed. They will even tell the victim this to their face and hold it over their head."

"But, does the victim ever catch on and defend themselves?" I asked.

"In a word, yes. The victim will eventually understand they are being sabotaged. But, by the time the victim realizes what is happening, it is too late for them to defend themselves. Their mutual friends are into the narce too deeply. Everyone will believe that the narce is the true origin of the victim's success. Mutual friends will withdraw from the victim and gather at the narce's side. There may be some stragglers, but for the most part, their expressions of belief in the victim will be stifled by the chaos and mess-making of the narce. No one will listen to the few who remain loyal."

"So, Frog, the narce will draw everyone they can to themselves and destroy the victim's reputation with those people. But doesn't the victim have anyone of influence on their side to rescue their reputation?"

"While it is reasonable to assume so, we must remember one thing. The narce has no boundaries. Their amoral code allows them to affect children, family members, church congregations, employers, and social clubs... no one is exempted. There are no relationships too sacred for the narce to destroy. The narce will try to leave the victim in total isolation, even as the victim speaks the truth to unbelieving ears.

"Speaking of 'sacred', narces will often adopt religion. At church, they may even use a façade of fake repentance to tell the church how they are oh-so-sorry for their past behavior. The narce is not above faking changes to make the victim believe that they have a common ground. The narce may even join a church under false pretenses to influence their victim and maybe to find other victims."

"That's just so… *cruel.*"

"Yes. But the narce's thirst for supplies is unlimited. The narce does not care about the victim's suffering. They actually relish in it."

"But why?"

"Because the narce also suffers, by no fault of the victim. The narce is secretly in terrible pain. They play out this way to make the victim suffer as well."

"It just makes no sense to me, my hopping friend."

"No, my bipedal friend. It makes no sense. In all my years, I have made no sense out of any of this. It is simply how narces work. They love to destroy the very things that could heal them because they hate themselves so much. They also hate the victim for loving them."

"What? That is so unreasonable."

"You are right. But we must remember that the narce is not a reasonable person. The narce suffers greatly because they don't believe they are worthy or good. Remember that at their very core, narces have terrible self-esteem and must create a false self to cover it up.

"Under the guise of the false self, which is 'perfect' in the narce's eyes, he believes that just being who they are justifies all that they do. They claim power over their victim and cause great suffering. Even as they do this, they suffer terribly behind that mask they wear. All the time, they pretend that they are doing this to demonstrate their superiority."

"Well, Frog, it has been most enlightening. Yet, I feel terrible."

"Well, go home, now and think things over. What you are feeling right now is a reflection of how terrible the narce feels. Don't dwell on those feelings because you may become depressed and not return to finish our project. That was how I lost John Steinbeck."

"You *knew* Steinbeck?"

"Indeed. Good night, George."

"Good night, Frog."

THE IMMEDIATE MENTAL HEALTH EFFECTS OF NARCE ABUSE

THE NEXT AFTERNOON, I appeared at the millstone. I did not see Frog. I waited and after about ten minutes, I started to worry. Then I saw a shower of yellow sparks and swirling energy. Frog suddenly appeared, floating in the water. He looked up, saw me, and was startled.

"Oh! Whoa! George! Um… you weren't supposed to see that."

"I wasn't supposed to see what? You appearing in the water in a shower of yellow sparks? Let's just say I am not surprised. What were you doing?"

"While we are 'just saying things', let's just say I had an errand to run, but now I am back. Don't bother asking again, because I cannot tell you."

"Fair enough! What are we to discuss today?"

"We will talk about the common thread which binds all narce relationships together."

"How can you bind different types of relationships together? Business is different from a mother's love. A mother's love is different from a friend."

"Yes, but relationships are all the same to the narce, because they do not feel anything good be on their own sense of entitlement. Don't get me wrong, they will feel differently about different people, but they won't feel differently about relating to them. Whether the relationship is in a business, a friendship, a religious type of bonding, or a romance, all narce relationships are run the same way. Each person is only a tool to the narce, to be used at their will and pleasure. All of the steps narces take in relationships are predictable."

"Predictable?" I started writing, the yellow sparks all but gone from my mind.

"There is the euphoria at first. This is the "love bombing" phase with the inherent overtures of respect, trust, love, and gifts. During this phase, the narce grooms the victim for destruction even as they are *oh, so kind*. This is a stage of investigation and discovery for the narce. The narce builds trust and confidence in the victim until they learn the weaknesses of the victim. What makes them happy? What makes them sad? What are their fears? This is a finding-out phase where the narce reveals so very little to the victim, even as the victim pours their heart and soul out to the narce who has earned their trust.

"After the narce has the victim fully committed to the narce, there comes the devaluation. The narce slowly wraps its coils around the victim's self-esteem and their belief in themselves and strangles it so very carefully. The victim will not and usually *cannot* believe what the narce is trying to do. No sincere person would believe that someone would be capable of doing such terrible things. Not unless they were educated on narcissism.

"The victim simply cannot believe what the narce is actually doing right under their nose. It just never occurs to them that people are capable of such deviousness. The narce whittles and chips, sands and saws, degrades and destroys the strength of the victim. The trusting victim will not see what the narce is doing to them because it is done slowly, insidiously, and with laser-focused intent. The victim just continues to love their trusted partner, friend, or associate, and *the narce sees that as a terrible weakness.*

"Then slowly, the victim starts to feel the effects of the abuse, of those strangling coils wrapped around their core. There are effects the victim suffers in the beginning, but they will never think that the suffering is caused by the narc. The victim will blame themselves or some other influence such as their true friends who are trying to protect them. The victim will often lash out against those who speak badly of the narc. The victim will actually stand up for the narc and tell the friends to back off and mind their own business.

"Friends who oppose the narc will not last long because the narc or even their victim will drive stronger friends away. During this phase, the narc is also winning the more easily influenced friends over to their side. The victim's friends begin to see the victim in a new and negative light. They begin to see the victim as inept, incapable, or in any other way the narc wishes. All the while, the victim is being strung along into trusting the narc more and more.

"These three power moves: weakening the victim, driving away strong friends, and influencing the victim's other friends all create the perfect situation for the narc. The stronger friends will be driven away by the narc, but the more malleable friends will be permitted to stay around for appearance's sake. People are less likely to be alarmed if a couple of the friends from the victim's old crowd are still around. That way, the change in the victim does not appear to be quite so profound.

"All the while, the victim buys more and more into the narc's game because they want to believe in the one they love and trust. All the while the victim is slowly changing psychologically. The victim is beginning to question their own intuition; they may even begin to question their own core beliefs. They are beginning to rely on the nice for all the answers to the tough questions. The narc is more than happy to provide the victim with 'all they need'.

"Eventually, the effects on the victim become self-evident. The victim is experiencing 'cognitive dissonance'. This is an internal conflict that occurs when a person's actions don't coincide with their own beliefs. The victim is doing what the narc wants to avoid punishment. The victim may even give up things they know are true to please the narc. The victim will actually do things that do not sit well with them, and that go against their core beliefs. The victim experiences great confusion at this time because they are betraying their very core and ignoring their intuition. This is all to please the narce who has broken the victim down.

"This is when the narce strikes. The narces wants to dismantle the victim's whole self-concept. The victim is being controlled and told *they are wrong about oh-so-many things.* The victim will start to give in more and more. The victim becomes mentally weary and depressed from continual internal conflict within themselves and the external conflict with the narce.

"The resulting exhaustion of the victim is not a sign of weakness. It is a sign of *normalcy!* Normal people are built up by love and harmony, but worn down by conflict and dissonance. The narce knows this and uses the conflict as fuel to gain more supply. *Conflict is literal fuel to the narce because they are energized by it!* For the narce, the more chaotic the relationship, the better.

"The narce will tell the victim's family and friends, their mutual acquaintances, and so on that the victim's ineptitude causes the conflict. They will blame the victim's inherent flaws and weaknesses for the failures they are having. The failures, by the way, are quite real. Financial trouble is one of the most common problems in narce relationships. Finances are often the first thing the narce takes over. Then, naturally, the financial troubles lead to other problems."

"But… the victim is not *actually* inept, is it?" I asked.

"Well, no, but… yes, they are at the same time."

"Huh?"

"Please allow me to explain. The victim is not naturally inept. The trouble, though, is that *the victim will actually starts to appear inept because they are slowly being destroyed inside.* The victim suffers from anxiety because of circular and unending narce arguments. It is draining them to have 'conversations' that never end until the victim 'admits' that something really *is* their fault, even when it is not. The victim will give in and admit fault because they want the endless fights to stop. Soon, the victim loses their ability to navigate conflict at all. Giving in becomes an easy shortcut for them because fighting for their right to autonomy is exhausting.

"The manipulation of the victim's mind by gaslighting, stomping on their feelings, constant beratement and browbeating causes the victim to lose faith in themselves. This is all topped off with the sly and underhanded remarks the narce casts at the victim privately and in public. All of these things take their toll. The narce does all of this in what they call 'conversations'. These so-called conversations are one-sided, destructive sessions of bending the victim's mind and will, all to broaden the narce's control.

"This 'gaslighting' I just mentioned is important. The name comes from an old movie, a psychological thriller. A man abused his victim by convincing her, his wife, that the gas light that illuminated their home was as bright as ever. But all the while he slowly turned the light down over time. The victim in the movie begins to doubt her own senses. The abusive husband twists her thinking so that she no longer believes she is sane. This movie portrays the goal of every narcissist: *They must make each victim doubt their own senses and their own sanity so they are dependent upon the narce in every one of their decisions. Mind control is the ultimate control. To capture the mind is to capture the person.*

"So, let me get back to the 'conversations', which are really arguments. These arguments will always end with a victory for the narce or with a false victory for the victim that the narce will later steal back. The victim will either be forced to admit it was their fault, or the narce will run them around in circles until they become so frustrated and angry that they simply walk out of the room. Then the narce will say 'You're angry with me? When this is your fault? See how unreasonable you are?' or 'Oh, yes. I see how you walk out on me all the time. You never want to talk things over.'

"The narce loves to draw the victim back in to try to win an argument that cannot be won. This is part of the wearing down of the victim's resolve. Getting the victim to reengage is an example of the 'hoovering' quality of the narce.

"Narces have another hoovering technique in the same vein. This is the false victory I just mentioned. The narce will allow the victim to 'win' an argument, particularly if the victim is threatening to leave the relationship. The win will allow the victim to believe that there is finally progress. Once the victim is comfortable again, the narce will take back the victory and restart the 'conversations'. These conversations are just the same old arguments and things never really change. The victim may believe there is progress, but the narce will take all of that back, eventually.

"During the 'conversations', the narce will repeatedly use the same old insults, scorns, yelling, cursing and negative references... whatever it takes. They know what will trigger the victim. They intentionally attack these psychic sore spots on the person. They keep hitting the old injuries over and over. We sometimes call this 'poking the bruise'. It is an underhanded technique that will work every time. After all, the victim is only human. A person will only stand so much prodding at an old injury, even if the hurt is emotional or symbolic.

"After the victim blows their cool, they believe they have lost the game. But really, the game was already lost before it ever began. The narce rigged the table, sanded the dice, trimmed and marked the deck, put a brake on the wheel, and won the support of the house dealers before they ever invited the victim in for a 'friendly game'. The victim will never win because the odds are not even real. Odds suggest a chance at winning the game."

"Well," I responded, "Even a crooked casino or carnival game has *some* winners, just by chance."

"A carny or casino dealer just wants your money and yes, by chance, they will lose once in a while. But the narce? Brother, I am here to tell you, *they never take a chance*! Anything you win is by their good graces and that win will just set you up for a greater loss. Remember that the narce wants to devalue you entirely. If they take only your money and leave you, it is much better."

"It is? Why?"

"Well, money can be regained. Things can be replaced. On the other hand, the devalued human being is a hard thing to reclaim. You see, the devaluation stage begins after the love bombing. The devaluation is done privately at first, then the narce becomes more public.

"In the beginning, the victim is confused by the narce's indifference when they are alone. They begin to question the narce's peculiar social habits. For instance, the narce may cut off or minimize communication. They may become dismissive of anything the victim says. They will contradict themselves.

"In social settings, the narce treats everyone better than the victim. The narce appears at their best and happiest when they are among other people. With time, the narce will start to talk about the victim with others. The narce begins the smear campaign, secretly. When the narce has figured out who is on their side, they become more open about it. They will even start to do this in front of the victim.

"To the unsuspecting victim, this is confusing, but tolerable at first. Then, after time, the victim starts to feel it. The victim starts to realize that they are being treated badly. By the time the victim feels the devaluation it is often too late. The victim cannot reclaim their good name because the narce has already spent considerable time wrecking their reputation.

"Then we have the narce's unpredictable moods. The victim is confused by narce's inconsistent response to situations. The victim never knows what the narce will think of their doing this or that. What was right yesterday is wrong today. What is true now, will be false later. Love this morning becomes indifferent in the evening. The victim starts to walk on eggshells and is always off-balance, in a state of doubt. When the doubt becomes powerful enough, the victim is ready to take the blame for everything that goes wrong… even when they are doing it right!"

"Wow," I said. "That is just awful."

"It is awful and it is destructive. This is more of the gaslighting we talked about earlier. The narce may contradict themselves in obvious ways but berates the victim when they bring it up. The narce tells them they are wrong about yesterday. That was never the narce's standard yesterday and the victim should know better than to think this today! *How dare you cross-examine me? How dare you question me, when you are clearly the problem!*

"To nurture the self-doubt, the narce will suggest that the reasons for their failures are because of the victim. They will tell the victim that their lack of poise, education, social skills, etc. are the cause of their mutual failure. They suggest that the victim is not as smart as the narce. The narce has more friends. The narce comes from a more educated and cultured background. Once the victim buys into this, the narce slowly begins to behave in a haughty, aloof manner. The victim does not wish for an argument and goes along with the narce's behavior. Soon, the narce's self-proclaimed superiority takes over the relationship. This is how the narce breaks their victim down."

"I see. Yes… I do see how this works." Then I thought of it for a moment. "We mentioned money, and how finances are easier to fix than a broken-down person. So, what about money? Money seems to be important the narce."

"Well, money represents power and the narce loves power. Despite that love affair with the power money represents, we see the narce being irresponsible with money. The victim often suffers financially due to the narce's impulsive, unpredictable spending. Financial difficulty is frustrating and depressing and is the perfect tool to keep the victim off-balance. It is particularly hard for the victim when they know that the narce's spending is intentional. This shows that narce loves the power that the abuse of money gives them over the victim.

"On the other end of the spectrum, the narce may also use financial pressure over the victim by hoarding money. The narce may claim that in the name of 'thrift' or 'frugality' that they should control the finances. They will then keep all the money to themselves, spending it as they see fit. Some narces will buy things for themselves, eat at restaurants, etc. while leaving the victim to do without.

"In any case of financial abuse, the victim will eventually realize that they are expected to give in to the narce's financial demands no matter what! The narce feels perpetually entitled to control the money. If the narce is an over-spender, then the victim should provide the money for them to do so. If the narce is a money hoarder, then the victim should provide the narce with the ability to hoard money. The victim should do so by never having a dime of their own and never complaining about it. They should give it all up to the narce, who is entitled.

"This is… it's just unbelievable."

"Yes. The whole thing is self-defeating, but it is what the narce wants. They want to cause pain. They love confusion. They get a thrill out of chaotic living. They want the victim to suffer in every way possible. They want drama to spread through their social circle. Most of all, they want to smell like a rose the whole time they are doing this.

Eventually, the victim will start to feel the effects of the abuse. When they consider ending the relationship, the narce gives them enough hope to stay in the relationship. When the narce senses that the victim is slipping from their grasp, they will back off the bad behavior. Then the victim thinks, 'This isn't so bad. They are getting over their mood.' As soon as the victim is hopeful, the abuse resumes. This cycle of hate, love, and hate will continue until the narce is ready to leave the victim. In our new jargon, this is a pattern of devalue, hoover, devalue, hoover, devalue… discard!

"Meanwhile, subject to the relentless abuse, gaslighting, and negative talk, the victim soon finds themselves in a position where they cannot trust anything in their life. They doubt themselves above all. Even in the self-doubt, the victim has hopeful feelings for the relationship. This hope bonds them to the narce in a traumatic way. They will constantly seek approval from the narce who feels no need to give that approval. When the narce does approve, it is merely to keep the victim in their place.

"Remember: *Everyone who understands and loves the victim will be systematically removed from the victim's life by the narce's treachery.* This puts the victim in a position of no support. They are now alone with their abuser. This isolation is intentionally caused by the narce who wants complete control of the victim. Only those people who are under the narce's spell are permitted to remain in the picture.

"When the victim experiences this behavior from a narce, it is real; yet the narce will tell everyone that the victim is imagining things. That is precisely what the narce wants everyone to think. The narce wants everyone to believe that the victim is deluded and will actually use the word 'crazy'. Remember that control is everything to the narce. If they can get control over the victim's mind or thinking, then they have control over the victim's whole person. This control is much easier to keep when the narce has control of the victim's social circle.

"But the victim still has a family, right?" I asked.

"Where family is concerned, the narce will either get control of the family and play them against the victim or they will drive the family away. The narce has no respect for the boundaries of other people. The narce believes themselves to be entitled to control over the victim's life. They will destroy, if possible, every other relationship in the victim's life. This includes family, friends, and anyone else who shows support for the victim. Many times, the narce will convince their victim that their family is no good for them.

"The victim is with the narce now, and that is all the victim needs. The narce will come with a laundry list of all the faults and failures of the victim's family, or whatever needs to be done. Meanwhile, the narce will make sure their own family stays completely in the picture. The narce is the ultimate dirty fighter. In establishing control of the victim, the ends justify the means."

"Okay, so control of the victim is the goal. Is this the same in all narce relations?"

"Yes. Ultimately, if successful, the only people the narce allows in the victim's life are people who believe in the narce. This gives supply to the narce for whom there is no such thing as a relationship for the sake of friendship or love. The narce either gets material benefits or other supplies out of their close associates. If there is no benefit or supply from having the person around, the narce will discard them," said Frog.

"But, certainly, this absolute control does not occur perfectly..." I said thoughtfully.

"No, it does not. People often are not easily controlled and the narce's success will be in varying degrees. There really is no such thing as 100%, absolute control over the victim at all times in all places. That is why the discard is so necessary and why the narce is continually planning for replacement supply."

"So, people who refuse to be controlled by the narce and leave, or who become boring, or simply run out of supply are discarded like old newspapers. That is very sad."

"Remember, too, that anyone who leaves is not only discarded but their reputation is ruined on their way out the door, if possible. Yes. Well, George, it is still early. Want to continue?"

"Sure."

1 2

PHYSICAL HEALTH EFFECTS OF NARCE ABUSE

"ALL RIGHT," began Frog, "Let's talk about the real physical health effects of narce abuse. It is no great secret that stress has physical effects. The most talked about are probably the diseases of the cardiovascular system. Hypertension, or 'high blood pressure' is called the 'silent killer' because many times, people who have it don't even know. Stress is a known cause of hypertension and this leads to a strain on the entire cardiovascular system. High blood pressure can lead to stroke, heart attack, and a numerous host of other problems.

"Stress can also cause stomach and digestive issues. Irritable Bowel Syndrome or 'IBS' can make a person's life miserable. Cramping, bloating, constipation, unpredictable diarrhea, and heartburn can wreck one's day and make sleep difficult. In the long run, these things can destroy a person's life.

"Now that I have mentioned sleep, we all know that stress alone can wreck our sleeping habits. Let me tell you that nightmares, night terrors, night sweats, insomnia, and general sleep disturbances are horrible for a person. When we cannot sleep properly, we become dull tools, ill-functioning, and emotionally dysregulated. These make for a difficult life during both the day and the night. The lack of restorative sleep will eventually cause severe psychological stress.

97

"Psychological stresses reflect in the body, as shown by IBS and hypertension. Migraines are often linked to psychological issues. Stress hormones, when overproduced, can cause inflammatory issues of all kinds of problems in the body. Joint pain, muscular issues, nerve and autoimmune disorders, blood sugar problems, and liver and kidney disease can many times be traced to stress.

"Certain stressors can even be linked to cancer. Everyone knows that stress and emotional turmoil can cause things like depression, post-traumatic stress disorder (PTSD), and a host of other mental maladies. Some less common manifestations of stress are out there, too. There is actually a type of *seizure* called a 'psychogenic non-epileptic seizure' (PNES)" that can be caused by certain stresses."

Frog stopped talking. He studied me for a moment. He let me finish writing. Then he said, "You seem puzzled. What is it?"

"I understand high blood pressure and PTSD," I said. "But seizures? How does mental stress cause seizures?"

"I see that I am getting ahead of you, George. Let me break it down for you: Psychogenic Non-Epileptic Seizure can be easily understood if we take the word a part at a time. Look at the roots of psycho (mind) genic (origin) non (not) epileptic seizure. Quite simply, this is a seizure that is caused by the mind but is not related to epilepsy. *These seizures are quite real but cannot be detected on an EEG.* The electroencephalogram will show 'normal' brain activity and yet, the patient has exaggerated shaking, spasms, dyskinesia, falling over, and so on. These seizures appear as though the person is having a serious medical problem.

"Although it is serious because the victim has lost control of their body, it is not as *dangerous* as it appears. It may seem that the person is not aware of their surroundings, but the fact is that they are thinking and speaking normally during these episodes. Sometimes, the PNES victims have hallucinations racing through their minds, and they describe what is going on in their heads.

"In spite of this, they still know who they are, where they are, and what is actually happening in their environment and they are oriented to the time of day. They may lose consciousness, but if they are awake, they are usually alert and oriented. This affliction can be very inconvenient and troublesome because these seizures come on without warning. They can range in duration from seconds to hours. They may involve one limb, just the head may bob, tremble, or twitch or the whole body may be involved.

"Since there is no apparent physical deformity or damage to the nerves, PNES is not usually controlled by medication with any great success. 'The wiring is fine, but the software is bad' one may say. Changing the victim's software, or their thoughts and emotional responses, is the most likely cure. Now, sometimes the victim of PNES might need meds or nutritional support to supplement cognitive (thought) therapy, but meds alone are not usually effective at controlling these.

"There is another illness related to stress that they like to call 'brain fog'. Confusion, lack of focus, forgetfulness, and low brain clarity are all found in 'brain fog'. This makes it very difficult for the patient to get by in a normal life, home, and work environment. Brain fog may come on and depart suddenly, or it can creep up slowly and become a long-term illness.

"Then there are the more well-known illnesses such as depression, anxiety, schizophrenia, and so on. These can all be situationally caused and symptoms will ease after things change. They may also be caused by some chemical imbalance the victim has from birth. The tricky part is that these may also be caused by any combination of situations, genetics, birth defects, and so on. Our main concern for this project is the situational stress caused by the narc.

"When any illnesses are caused by situational stress, they are grouped under the term 'psychosomatic' illnesses. This refers to illnesses caused by the mind. We must understand that *even though these illnesses are caused by the mind it does not make them any less real.* The mind becomes stressed and the patient will suffer. The suffering is real and the illnesses are real. These illnesses can be reversed in many cases when the victim starts to overcome the negativity that causes them.

"Remember that the narce loves drama, anger, and arguing. They are poorly regulated in emotions and their expression. In other words, the narce is out of control and generally terrible to get along with. The empath cannot stand this. They are easily affected by such negativity. This is why empaths in particular are so prone to the psychosomatic illnesses that we have discussed.

"Empaths deeply feel the narce's rage and angst, and then become convinced that they are somehow at fault. This causes the empath to continually, obsessively ruminate about ways they can please, help, or 'fix' the narce. The empath has no time for themselves to recover from the damage that the narce is doing to them. Remember, too, that the narce has usually isolated their victim from all sources of outside help.

"As the empath suffers emotionally and is without support, the suffering causes mental and physical symptoms. No matter how 'strong' the empath appears on the outside, their mind and body are breaking. Generally speaking, empaths feel the need to appear strong because they don't want to cause others stress or unhappiness from worrying about them. This empathic behavior trait gives the narce an ever-increasing foothold in the life of the empath. The greater the foothold, the greater the suffering. This can even extend to physical abuse during the relationship.

"We often hear of the 'beaten wife/partner syndrome', or how the abused make excuses for the abuser. This is how deeply narce control can affect people. It is very common for an abusive parent, either the father or the mother, to exercise total control over a family. When the control and sickness run deeply enough, financial, mental, emotional, social, and physical abuse all come into play.

"People want to believe that it is the man who is always the abuser, but there was a case written in the book *A Boy Called 'It'*, where the mother was the abuser. The father was a fireman, a very *macho* and heroic type of job. Even so, the fireman was being abused by the wife. He was so defeated and sickened emotionally that he could not stand up to his narce abuser wife, though he clearly saw what was happening to their son.

"The laws in those days were written in such a way as to prevent the boy from being taken away and the parents prosecuted. Eventually, the boy survived only because some school officials and a cop broke some laws and got the boy out of the situation. These people risked their own careers in doing so. The boy would have died without their brave intervention."

"But, Frog," I interrupted, "why would the narce want the *empaths* to be sick? Why would they physically abuse them? The victims could, as you say, even die from such stresses."

"Remember how we spoke of the narce's view on the victim's suicide? This is exactly the same thing. The narce view is 'If the victim suffers and dies, then, well, so be it. That just proves I was right.' The narce will put on a big show and just drink in the sympathy of being a widow or widower. The weeping, the funeral, the grave, the sorrow, the tears, and so on will be a great supply.

"Remember that the narce constantly searches for a new supply to take over where the old supply had the nerve to leave off by dying. And no… this is not an exaggeration. If you want to see an example of using death for sympathy, the movie *The Sixth Sense* tells the story of a little girl ghost who appears to a psychic boy, asking for his help. She was poisoned by her mother and now her sister is sick from the same thing. The mother poisoned the girls to collect sympathy and supply from their illness and death."

"I have seen that movie, Frog. I am surprised that you watch movies," I smiled.

"I hear about them from people, George. I cannot go into a theater. Remember… I am but a frog with limitations."

"Right… right… sometimes I forget that while we are talking."

"Getting back to our lesson… It is vital to you understand that *the narce actually will blame the dead for dying, for being too weak to live.* The fact that the narce survives is evidence to them in their sick world that the empath was the weakling the entire time. The narce will weep on the outside to show the world, but will privately gloat on the inside. This is how sick the narce's world actually becomes, over time, and-- Oh… my… Are you with me, George? You okay? You look a little pale."

"Yes, Frog," I swallowed hard. "This is all terribly hard to digest. The idea that the narce may cause death and then blame the victim for being too weak to live… is difficult. May I be excused until tomorrow?"

"Yes, of course," said Frog with concern in his eyes. "This was the last of this lesson, anyway. We may resume tomorrow. I know that this is hard for you, George. It is hard because you have lived and know some of these truths. Get some rest and come back in the morning."

13

LOVE BOMBING

T{\sc he next day} came and I had recovered from the shock of the recent learning. Frog was delighted to see me and after a couple of probing questions concerning my state of mind, he continued with the lessons. He wanted to go over something today that was not quite so heavy and dark.

"We have talked a bit about 'love bombing', and it is time to explain this more fully. Love bombing is a wildly manipulative and highly effective narce technique. The narce will literally 'bomb' the empath with 'love'. Their actions will be so over the top that the victim will be bowled over. They will be constantly, pleasantly surprised by gifts and considerate gestures. They will be stunned by how much they are loved. People who understand narce behavior will not fall for the love bomb because something will seem 'off' about it all. It will seem a little *too* perfect.

"The empath who does not know any better will fall for it every time. The narce does feel the intense euphoria of their own love bomb, and the empath feels this in the narce. The problem is that the euphoric feelings are not for the victim. The intense love and thrill the narce feels are for their new supply. The narce found a new person to manipulate and destroy. This is the why the narce feels happy.

"The victim may feel that something is a 'little off here and there', but they will chalk it up to their own imagination. They will ignore the evidence because they will feel the euphoria and interpret that as 'love'. They will believe that the narce loves them as much as the empath loves the narce! Nothing could be further from the truth.

"The victim will believe they have their soul mate and will love them with a tender passion that is deeply profound and unmistakable. The victim will be taken in hook, line, and sinker. The victim will believe that the narce is as loving and giving as they are. No one will be able to convince the victim that they are wrong because in their case, love truly is blind. It is blind to the manipulation, backstabbing, ill will, selfishness and all else the narce is actually going to offer.

"The narce already knows that their victim will serve them when the love bombing is over. Once the devaluing stages begin, the victim will do anything they can to win back the narce's euphoric 'love'. The victim will hope that the narce will return to being happy. They will work very hard to please the narce and bring back the love. The trouble is that 'the love' never existed. There never was love.

"The narce was manipulating their victim, learning about them. The narce was gauging how gullible the victim was this whole time. They learned what made their victim tick. They learned how the victim responded to words and deeds. The narce learned how to read their victim and carried them to great heights, prepping them for the monstrous crash and burn.

"On the other side of this exchange, the empathic victim is sincere in their love. They would never believe that these overt 'love bombing' actions of sacrifice and adoration are all fake. The victim cannot believe that the narce is only in this thing for the supply. It simply never occurs to them that a person could be so viciously disingenuous. To the empath, the narce's love bombing seems natural because this is the kind of over-the-top love that the empath believes in."

"Okay, Frog. I understand that the narce is being phony. That part is abundantly clear. So now I have to ask about this 'supply' you keep talking about. What is it?"

"I will answer that if you are okay to continue."

"Yes, Frog, I feel fine and may continue. The love bomb lecture was short. You just reviewed something I already understood, anyway."

14

SUPPLY

FROG STUDIED me for a moment and then decided that, yes, I could keep going.

"Very well, then. There is considerable debate about what 'narce supply' actually is. The uncertainty lies in what to actually name the motivational factor behind a narce's actions. One thing we know for sure is that the narce is continually seeking some kind of satisfaction. We also know that when they do receive satisfaction or even total fulfillment, it is never long-term.

"The narce will make 'friends' that seldom last. They will seek to have everyone's attention, all the time. The limelight must always be trained on the narce. Once they are in the spotlight, they must generate more excitement. When the excitement runs out and the people around them fail to produce proper adoration, adventure, money, etc., the narce will dump these people. It does not matter who they are, including family members.

"Bear in mind, too, that not all narce relationships will always be short-term. The narce may also keep a wonderfully empathic supply around them in the form of a spouse or other long-term romantic interest. Now, for that romantic partner to last with the narce, the partner must be a never-ending source of supply. Maybe they have wealth. Maybe they have looked. Or maybe a boyfriend or girlfriend provides the narce with some form of long-term amusement. Maybe the narce is married and playing a love triangle game. The supply could be anything.

"Remember that drama and emotional tension are a huge boost for the narce. They thrive on drama and chaos. They love to see things going badly because they love to watch suffering. They will produce problems, dilemmas, and situations that cannot be resolved. They will do all they can to stir up people and wreck lives.

"They will even do things not in their interest, and then blame another for the results of their ill-advised actions. They will spread the word far and wide about how their friend, lover, spouse, or whomever just simply ruined every-thing and wrecked their lives. By all appearances, the situation should be one that the narce would want to resolve. But the narce won't want a solution because of the attention, drama, and tension it creates. The narce lives for such conditions.

"In the end, it does not matter what 'supply' the narce craves. They will find a way to get it and won't stop until they do. It does not matter who they have to harm to get their supply, even though their satisfaction is short-lived.

"So, we can safely say that narcissistic supply is whatever the narce needs at the moment. That is why the narce is so hard to understand. That is why they are impossible to please. That is why they only want people around them who give them supplies. And this is why long-term friends are rare. Or if there are long-term friends, they are never terribly close to the narce. The friends may think that they have known the narce for fifteen years. The truth is that they never truly knew them. They may have *known something about* the narce, but really, they have been falling for the façade for fifteen years.

"If the friends are honest, they will have to say that no, they really did not know the narce. All they knew was what the narce presented to them. In real-ity, the narce's needs are superficial and ever-changing. This is why it is so exhausting for the families of narces. They cannot keep up with the demands and the changes."

I stopped writing and pondered for a long minute. Frog let me contemplate this complex idea. Then I responded, "So, supply is whatever the narce wants it to be. It defies definition and description because it is a… well, a wild card. It changes with the mood of the moment."

"That is a good way to put it, George. Supply is simply whatever the narce is seeking at the time. Nothing more, nothing less."

"Very good, Frog. Well, I am going to stop here, if that is okay. I want to spend some time going through these notes."

"Okay, George. Next time, we will talk about vampires."

"Okay, Frog. You are becoming quite the kidder, you know," I chuckled lightly.

"We shall see. Farewell," Frog smiled knowingly.

15

VAMPIRISM

THE NEXT DAY, I found Frog just floating in the water, enjoying the sun. I was surprised at how attached I was becoming to this situation. Frog was my mentor and my friend. Though I knew this had to end one day, I hoped it never would.

"Good day, Frog! I am here to learn about 'vampires'," I chuckled again at the thought.

"Hail, friend! Have a seat on the millstone. I will tell you all about vampires now."

"So… you weren't kidding."

"Nope. If your pen is ready, so am I. This term 'vampire' is precisely what you think it is. We are generally familiar with the horror movie Vampire. The vampire, or 'vamp', is a creature that lives on the blood they draw from another's veins. The vampire legend was inspired by the life and times of a horrifically cruel dictator, named Vlad the Impaler."

(Note to the Reader: If you are particularly sensitive, skip the italicized paragraph below.)

"Vlad would order prisoners, slaves, and innocent people to be dropped onto a sharply pointed stake set into the ground. The stakes were tall and quite sturdy. They were several inches in diameter. The dropped person would be pierced through the torso by the stake, and their body would slide down the length of the pole as far as it could. The victim would squirm and scream until they finally lost consciousness and died. These victims were left to decompose on the stakes as a psychological deterrent to Ottomans who were pursuing Vlad's army.

"The cruelty of Vlad is reflected in the blood-sucking horror icon, Count Dracula. The horror of both Vlad and Dracula is reflected in the narce. The truly malignant narce would have no problem with tormenting a victim to death. Such cold people do exist. Just like Vlad the Impaler, they will unjustly punish innocent people. They do this just to watch them suffer and squirm. They will make also make the suffering of the victim very public, for all to see.

"Plus, all while, similar to Dracula, *a narce draws the precious life force from their victim by taking power over them and keeping them close.* Both Dracula and the narce are charming and keep terrible secrets about their weaknesses and insecurities. Narce secrecy is comparable to the Dracula story because very few people believe that Dracula was taking victims' blood and few will believe that the narce is taking their victim's life away. Other similarities include the hypnotic power of the vampire and the trauma bonding of the narce and their victim. Both powers cause the victim to stay with their tormentor even though life is being sucked out of them.

"Vampires and narces also have certain things that weaken them. The symbol of the Christian cross is intolerable to the vampire. Actual love and sacrifice are intolerable to the narce, who cannot understand such things. Dracula needed dirt from his native country to sleep upon or he would perish. The narce needs the constant supply of perceived perfection in themselves to get through the day and night. The vampire will dry out and be reduced to ashes in the sunlight while the narce will be reduced to ash by the light of truth. Do you see now the parallels between the selfishness of the vampire legend and the actual, real being of the narce?"

"Um… well… yes I do! That is an incredible parallel, all right. Dracula is the ultimate narce and has Achilles' heels that he needs to avoid just like the narce! Not only that but both vamps and narces take victims from the living and destroy all that is good in their lives!"

I was excited and horrified at the same moment by all of this.

"Yes, George! You see now! We have discussed already the physical, psychological, and psychosomatic pains and illnesses that the narce will cause in their victim. The victim's life changes completely, ever so slowly. The whole time the narce is carefully guiding and likely brainwashing them into believing that they have the victim's best interest at heart. The narce will promise a better life of light and joy. But like Dracula, after their work is done, the narce will deliver only darkness, destruction, servitude, and even death.

"I will explain how it works as clearly as I can: Healthy relationships carry on with both parties loving and supporting one another. They do so via giving and receiving. These efforts increase one another's life-energy resources and positivity. Each person gives and receives again and again. They grow together, each seeking their partner's best interest in an upward spiral. The partners are true partners in every sense of the word. They improve one another and each becomes their own best self as the relationship flourishes. Then together, they create a whole that is greater than the sum of their parts.

"In the narce relationship, the victim believes the narce's pretty words and promises. The victim believes they have a relationship, so they want to grow into a better person along with their partner. Down the road, though, instead of growing, the victim suffers from mental and physical exhaustion. The narce draws out of the victim all of the light and energy that they can.

"The victim gives, gives, and gives while the narce takes… and takes… and takes… The more they take, the darker things become for the victim. The victim hangs on, though, hoping that the narce will one day keep their word. The narce never returns love or support unless they know it is somehow going to supply the long run.

"The problems in the relationship will never be resolved unless the narce matures emotionally. The problem is that there is no maturity or growth for the narce. There is no changing them. They don't see the point, so why bother? *For the narce, there is no need to change. There is only the supply they receive from the victim.* The narce has no truly equal partner in their mind. This is because no one is good enough to match the narce's ideal image of what a partner would be.

"Throughout the relationship, the cycle continues. The victim keeps giving and pleasing, trying to make it work and hoping that the narce will change. The change never comes, other than to quickly provide a few breadcrumbs of hope when the victim threatens to leave. The narce gives the victim just enough hope to hoover them back into the old patterns.

"Soon, as you probably imagine, the victim is depleted of all of their energy. The energy is being sucked out of them by a real energy vampire. This is a literal thing, not just some silly metaphorical idea. The victim in the narce relationship literally has very little energy to live on. They are so tired in mind and body from the constant conflict, chaos, and drama that they just cannot properly refresh, restore, and regenerate their spirit.

"The victim now has trouble keeping up at work, school, or both. They become cranky, withdrawn, and unpleasant. The victim begins to break down. The narce continues to tear the victim down behind their back. The narce tells everyone that it is oh-so-hard to live with the cranky, solemn victim. The narce enjoys tormenting their victim, even as they collect additional supplies from the friends and family who feel sorry for the poor narce.

"After a while, the victim becomes confused and foggy of mind, unable to so much as think straight. Because of this, they may do stupid things simply because they no longer have the energy or common sense to avoid mistakes. The victim will appear displeased with life, or maybe just 'bland' or 'blah'. Soon, they will not socialize because the narce will just put them down in front of company or drive friends away from the victim. When the narce and their victim are at a party or some other gathering, the narce will have the time of their life! Meanwhile, the victim just sits there, dull-looking, and seems unwilling to communicate.

"Others may approach the victim, but the victim will seem to be content to not join the party. This is because the narce will just criticize them at home later, and speak poorly of their lack of social skills and of how ungraceful they appear. The victim is constantly being taught by the narce that they are not worthy, or not in the same class as the narce and their friends, or that everyone else at the party has accomplished great things while the victim has not. The victim's lack of accomplishment is an embarrassment, after all. *For shame!*

"After a while, the victim will not be able to supply the narce with what they want because the victim is simply drained. They cannot go anymore. They may beg, plead, or cry, but these pleadings and tears do not impress the narce. The victim's feelings and desperation simply do not matter. All the while, the narce is pleased and their ego is fed by the victim's suffering.

"Once the narce is no longer getting supply, whatever it may be, then the narce discards the victim. They dump the victim hard, unceremoniously, and for all the world to see. A narce will literally ruin their victim and put them on the street, glad to see them suffer.

"After the discard, like Dracula grooming new victims, the narce will turn to their new supply and tell the new supply how big of a failure the old supply was. The new, fresh supply will certainly understand why the narce cast off the old supply. After all, what good was the old supply? They could not even keep themselves off the streets. What business did they have trying to be with the narce, who is *obviously* in a higher, superior class of person?

"The new supply will not realize they are being used. The narce will make the new person feel like a million bucks. The narce will tell the new one how much better they were than the old supply. The narce will be oh-so-happy with the new one. They will make all kinds of excuses for why they had to leave the old relationship and take up with this new person.

"The narce will build up in the minds of all their new people an image of life with the old supply. The narce will always talk about how they reached down and tried to help the old supply. They will talk about how the old supply ignored the narce's best advice. The old supply was always stubborn and mean. The old supply was abusive and terrible to be around.

"Oh, the narce tried *so hard to help* but eventually had to leave the old supply to their own devices. The narce will say the old supply failed to live up to what the narce knew they could do. The old supply just simply failed at life overall. The narce will say that it was the victim's own fault. *Alas! If only the victim had lived up to the narce's reasonable expectations…* and so on.

"It is hard to say, George, how many of the people who litter the streets were victims of narce abuse. How many geniuses will never be recognized? How many books, songs, and poems will never be written? How many inventions will never see the light of day? How much beauty and honor will never be known to the world, all because a narce took advantage of a compassionate man or woman and ruined them?"

"Frog… it is hard to guess. I will say, though, that I will never look at homeless people the same ever again. It is well to know these things, Frog."

"And I am glad to teach you. Shall we continue?"

"If you have the time, I have the pen."

"So be it. Are you familiar with a well running dry?"

16

THE NARCE'S IDEAL

"FROG," I began, "before we speak of wells, I think we glossed over something important. You mentioned something about the narce's 'ideal image'. Something about the partner. I have it here in my notes…"

"Oh, yes! I am glad you brought that up. We have talked a lot about the supply that the narce craves and how they torment the victim. We have talked about victim blaming and how the narce tells everyone it is the victim's fault that the relationship ended. Have you wondered how the narce rationalizes it all?"

"Well, I gather that the narce has the false self they present to the world. The false self is different from what the victim sees in private. The false self is different from whoever sees it. The narce shows the person who is in front of them what they need to see to adore the narce."

"Yes, good so far."

"The narce craves all of this attention and supply and cannot live without it."

"Correct."

"But, we have never talked about the 'rationalization' piece. Usually one rationalizes when they are potentially troubled about something they have done or intend to do."

"Yes."

"Okay, we know the narce is void of conscience, so why would they need to rationalize?"

"Very astute question! Yes, George, you are finally getting to the bare bones of the narce. They do not have a conscience, not in the way a normal person does, and certainly not in the way an empath does."

"Then why rationalize?"

"They need the ultimate excuse. They need a trump card that can explain all of their meanness and all of their actions toward the victim. Most of the victim's suffering is never known to the world. The world has no idea what the narce has actually done to the victim. The world knows the victim through the narce's eyes only. The few people who know the truth are simply dismissed from the narce's circle because the narce cannot tolerate the truth."

"So, the narce has a type of 'get out of jail free card' that they can present to the world. They can explain what happened and why the relationship had to fail."

"Yes. While the narce does not really care about what they did, they must have a way to explain to the world what they did and why."

"Got it. And what would that 'get out of jail free' card be?"

"It's very simple. I call it 'the narce's ideal'."

"Ideal what?"

"Their ideal mate, friend, partner, neighbor, etc."

"And what would that be exactly?"

"That, George, is the golden question. What would that be, indeed. Well, it is very simple. The narce has their false self that they show everyone, yes? Well, the narce also has a false *you*."

"A *what*? A false *me*? How is that even possible?"

"It's not possible. But it is how the narce gets out of jail free, as you put it."

"Wait… a false me… Don't tell me. Let me work it out… A false me. Since the narce wants me to fail for the sake of the attention and supply, they cannot allow me to succeed. They make me fail by sabotaging my efforts, by getting in my way. They make me fail by intentionally doing things that stop me from succeeding. In their eyes, success is not our having joy and prosperity. *Narce success is only that which gives them supply…*"

"Very good, George. You are almost there…"

"They receive supply from having all the attention on themselves. They use others to get attention. They crave whatever supply is needed at the moment. They want fame, glory, honor attention. They will blame the partner for failure… Wait… That's it! *When the partner does not live up to whatever the narce needs to get supply, they will claim that supply anyway by making the relationship fail!* The chaos of the breakup becomes the new supply! That's it! *Right there! It is all about the narce.*

"I think I have it, now. The narce wants the victim to be this or that way, so the narce has the limelight. The narce wants to be responsible for the victim's success. They build up an image of what they want that partner to be. The partner must be this or that and perfect in this and that way, to provide the supply for the narce! The narce is all about using the partner to build up and aggrandize themselves!

"The narce believes that the victim should become the narce's ideal, 'for the victim's own good.' But the narce wants their ideal, whatever that may be, for their own supply. It is not for the victim to shine. They want the victim to provide supply by living up to the narce's ideal of who the victim should be! If the victim manages to somehow become the narce's ideal, then the narce will take all the credit. They will then have gobs of supply flowing in."

"Ah! Excellent! Now can you think of an example?"

"Well… Let's say that a woman wants to be married to a fireman. She will find a man who has a suitable physique for it. He will express an interest in emergency medicine and response. She will love-bomb that man and dupe him into believing he is her 'one and only'. She will promise to be whatever it is that will make him happy. She learned what to say during her grooming and love bombing.

"She will pretend that she wants this and that for their marriage. She builds that all-important fake future. They get along famously. They are oh-so-great together. She expresses how happy she is and how wonderful he is.

"Then let's say that something disqualifies him from the hiring process. Something that is not his fault stops him from making the grade. He has some malady or training injury that affects him and he cannot become a fire-fighter, ever. Since he has failed to become her ideal man, she devalues him, degrades, crushes his self-image, shows everyone that he is broken, and leaves him. All of this done without remorse."

"Yes. That is a very simple way to express it. You have captured the essence of the moment. You have proven a deep understanding of a complex topic and expressed it in a highly comprehensible way. You have shown in that quick story the love bomb, the fake future, the manipulation, the need for supply, the devaluation, the victim blaming, discard… all of it. I think that you do understand what we have been talking about."

"Thank you, Frog. Now I would like to learn about the well running dry."

"So, you shall."

17

DRAINING THE WELL

"You see, George, the narce will take all of what the victim has to give and will use it up. They will cast any unusable remnants aside. Then the narce will put their hand out for more. We all know that wells are holes that contain life-giving water. Water is precious. Life cannot exist without it. We need to be careful with water because it takes a while to refill the well.

"Now let's apply this to the narce relationship. A narce will take all of the life-giving substance the victim has to offer and will just waste it. They have no plan for replenishment, no idea of how to get by, and no idea of how to correct the problems they caused. They just drain the victim's life-giving well and then demand that the victim replenish it.

"All of the money, all of the means, all of the influence, and all of the friends and family that the victim brings into the equation will simply disappear. The narce brings nothing to the relationship of any value. They will claim that they have value, oh yes. They may even show that they have value in some way or another, during the love bombing stage. The narce will show off what they have and prove their value.

"Then, once the love bombs stop dropping, the narce entirely changes their tune. The narce will slowly or perhaps abruptly stop producing. They will take everything the victim has. One of the very first things the narce will do is to begin to take over all finances. They will try to exclude the victim from control over money. It may seem like a small thing, at first. In the long run, though, the victim cannot spend even small amounts without the narce's permission. The narce, of course, spends whatever they like. This is a deeply degrading form of abuse.

"Remember that the narce must control the victim as a whole. It starts with money. Then they take away all of the victim's confidence as they chip away at the victim's belief in themselves. The narce will remove family and friends from the victim's life by convincing the victim that their family is not good for them and they need 'better' friends. The victim's true friends and family will never be good enough. The narce wants all friends and family to support the narce, no matter what.

"We must remember this key element: *The narce considers no relationships as off limits or too sacred to destroy.* According to the narce, the well of life that the victim brought to the relationship belongs to the narce, now. It does not matter if this is fair or not. The narce is so entitled and spoiled that they will actually believe that they DESERVE all the victim has. They also believe that the victim deserves nothing, including friends.

"Because of their entitled mentality, the narce does not hesitate to take everything and show no mercy to the victim. Whatever the victim has will end up in the narce's hands, if they get their way. The narce has no problem leaving the victim penniless, friendless, and shattered.

"They will also try to take the victim's good name and reputation. There will be nothing left for the victim if the narce's victory over them is complete. Yes, *victory.* The narce wins only by causing a loss for the victim. The narce wants to deplete the victim's well of life-giving resources.

"The most tragic thing is that the victim had no idea that they were being drained. They did not know that this relationship was all about the narce sucking them dry. But the narce knew. Oh, yes! The narce knew what they were after. They were out to take this person's resources and claim them as their own!

"Even though my teachings seem to lean toward romantic and family relationships, the same rules apply to friendships, businesses, and even religious relations. The only reason the narce enters a relationship is to draw from the other's well. The narce's favorite victims will succumb to the whims of the narce, trying to please them, even as they lose all that they have.

"The hardest part for the victim recovering from a narce relationship is to reclaim their vital life-giving resources. The victim will have to return to family and repair broken relationships if they can. The victims will have to learn to love themselves again if they ever did in the first place. They will have to replenish their well one painful drop at a time. It will be difficult, yes, but if the victim really tries, they can work things out.

"They must accept, too, that sometimes there is no recovering that lost water. Their well may not ever be the same again, with so much time and love lost. The victim must learn to accept that this is actually 'okay'. The victim must realize that they will, with effort and help, emerge all the stronger.

"In reference to the victim's resources, we may take the term 'life-giving' and change it to 'love-giving'. To normal people, life is found in love. Love-giving resources must be sought by the victim for them to recover. All is not lost if the victim still has love to give. It may be hard for the victim at first to receive and accept fully the love that is offered to them. They will have to break a lot of old, self-deprecating habits.

"The degree of difficulty experienced during the victim's recovery will depend on how much damage the narce did to them during the relationship. The main thing is that the victim must accept the lessons they have learned. They must accept that they can actually go on to live the light-filled life they were meant to have." Then Frog simply stopped talking. I finished my notes.

"Frog, that is the most profound thing I have ever heard. I have never before realized that love is our life-giving reserve. It all makes so much sense. I have concluded now that the reason the narce clamors for supply is that they somehow interpret their supply as their life force. They are devoid of true love, so they must have supply."

"And this, George, is the essence of this entire project. Pure love is the true life-giver. Because pure love cannot fail. Love is the only thing in our lives that grows as we give it away, passing it back and forth. As we give and receive, it only grows into something bigger than we ever thought. We become better, brighter, stronger, and more compassionate. Our well, or our cup, if you prefer, will overflow as we give and receive."

"I thought for a moment and responded with, "That means that love is an everlasting resource. Supply, then, must be a limited resource because the narce uses it all up on themselves. They never give it to another. They must constantly work to claim supply."

"Ahh... yes... you are starting to see, finally!" said Frog, apparently overjoyed.

"If supply is a finite resource, does that... yes. Yes, it does!"

"It does what?"

"It means that *the narce must constantly seek supply because they run out of it so quickly. That means they will compete for it if it is not freely given!"*

"Yes, they must. I am very excited about your progress, George! Now listen to this..."

I sat back, pen in hand, waiting for this next lesson. It was going to be a great lesson, for certain. I simply knew that it must be!

18

NARCISSISTIC COMPETITION

"It is very interesting to me that you discovered the depth of the competition factor of narcissism all on your own. We alluded to it in an earlier lesson, and you managed to run with it just now. That took some insight. I think we chose you wisely."

"Thank you, Frog. I want you to know that I have healed, too, during this journey."

"Yes. Much to your credit you have accepted and absorbed my teachings into your person. Now, getting back to the competitiveness… The narce is always running out of supply because they do not feel loved. They may be loved by others, true, but they do not feel loved. They do not feel worthy of love. They conclude, out of self-defense that love does not exist. They also conclude out of self-defense that supply is their life-giving force, not love.

"The narce knows that their supply runs out quickly. They know that to them, supply makes them 'feel good'. Without supply, they are left on their own, feeling terrible, because for whatever reason they reject love. They don't feel it and they don't receive it. The pain that would be required for them to receive love is just awful and they don't want to face that."

"But, Frog, where would the pain come from?"

"The pain comes from vulnerability. To show vulnerability is to admit that they need others. This causes them pain. They want to be the ultimate source of their own happiness because they don't believe in love. They believe that the only one they can actually count on is themselves."

"That cannot possibly work. That attitude is so selfish and happiness cannot be found in selfishness."

"You are correct. They have the choice to not be selfish. If they admit that they are less than perfect, they are vulnerable and vulnerability causes them great pain. We may never know why this is, but the narce cannot accept that pain. Perhaps it is foolish pride. In any case, their reasons and motives are just not important to us. Right now, we are learning to defend ourselves from such people.

"To protect ourselves we must first understand our enemy. To understand the narce, we must learn how they think about supply. They believe that they deserve supply. They must have a supply. They cannot live without it. They will do whatever they must to gain that all-important element that keeps them alive. They, as you said, compete for it because it is a finite resource.

"Competition is in everything the narce does. They must beat you. They find supply in the victory when no one else even knew there was a race. The race is for the narce's supply. They will run someone over, pin them down, and extract it from them. Whatever the narce craves, they will take it just a like a mugger seeking drug money.

"The narce will compete continually for attention, for affection, for money, for the spotlight, and anything else. That is why they crave control. They want to keep everyone in their place, in a position to provide their 'fix' of supply. The narce is an addict, remember that. They will stop at nothing to get what they are after.

"Love, remember, is a give-and-take proposition. Competition is a take-and-take proposition. Competition is the only thing that interests the narce. They will take and take, creating in their path a flood of victims. They will always find victims, too, among normal, loving healthy, light-filled people.

"Normal people generally want good for others. They want to do good for others. They want to have happy and fulfilled lives. Know that the narce is not happy and is not fulfilled. The only fulfillment they have is their life source of temporary supply. That is why they compete. They compete, literally, with everyone in their lives.

"Narce parents will compete no matter what the station is in life: Parents will compete with children over who is smarter or better looking. Siblings will compete with siblings over who is the worthier child. Coworkers will compete for the attention of the boss. Bosses will compete with their subordinates to keep them in their assigned roles so they cannot advance. There is no loyalty, there is no true giving or selflessness with the narce. They will destroy others, if they must, to have their supply.

"In romantic relationships, it is this drive to compete that keeps their victim out of the spotlight. The narce will claim that they want their loved one to grow. They do want their partner to grow, yes, but only in a way that will keep the narce in the spotlight. If the narce cannot steal the credit for 'building' the victim's success, they will destroy whatever it is at which the victim has become successful.

"I mentioned parents a moment ago, and there is a point I would like to make about narce parents, specifically. In family relationships, narce parents will jealously prevent their children from becoming anything that would compete with the parent's supply. For instance, if a parent was a medic in the military, then if one of the kids becomes an EMT, the parent will mock and degrade the child's efforts. The parent will jealously guard the supply they get from telling their medical/combat stories. They won't want the child to have their own stories to compete with the parent, thus sharing the spotlight."

"Yes, Frog, I get it. The narce cannot share the spotlight. What a dark, selfish, and terrible way to live."

"Yes, it is dark. Interestingly, you bring up the darkness. We are going to talk now about 'going dark', even as we try to reclaim our lives from the narce. Don't worry, it is not what you think. Shall I continue?"

"Yes, Frog. I am able."

"Good."

19

DISCARD AND 'GOING DARK'

"WE HAVE MENTIONED 'DISCARD' a couple of times. Notice that we are not calling this a 'breakup' or a 'rejection'. We call it a 'discard' for a reason. The word itself may conjure up images of simply dropping a playing card on the table, or casually tossing away a bit of refuse without another thought. This is an apt description of how the narce feels about a breakup.

"When they initiate the breakup, it is done without *any* remorse on the part of the narce. *The victim must understand the narce never feels remorse or regret.* As hard as it may be for the victim, they must understand *the narce did not, does not, and will not ever care about the victim. The victim never mattered to the narce. The victim was just another tool that had lost its usefulness. The person that the victim knew and loved did not exist. That person they knew and loved was the narce's façade, the narce's false self.*

"The discard will usually be incredibly painful for the victim because the victim was *carefully groomed and chosen for their ability to forgive and care no matter what!* The victim will usually not really believe that the relationship is over. They will believe that the narce does not mean it when they lash out to break the relationship. The breakup does not make any sense because the façade they love would never do such a thing. The trouble is that while the façade would not, the narce *just did.*

129

"When it is time for the discard, justice and fairness do not enter the equation. The narce feels no remorse. The narce has no awareness of, or concern for, what is fair and what is not. They will not care if the discard 'makes sense' or not. The narce truly said and means that the relationship is over. The narce will finally tell the truth at the discard: *They never really cared for their victim from the beginning.* Perhaps the narce may not say that openly, but they will show it to the victim by their actions. The victim will then see that the narce never did have any regard, much less love, for the victim.

"The victim will suffer terribly, because they do care. They will instinctively try to cooperate with the narce. The victim will want to be reasonable and will want the breakup to be amicable and fair. This is especially true if children are involved. If the victim wants to be fair, that is fine with the narce. They will use the victim's sense of fair play to get what they want. What is it they want? *Everything.*

"The narce has manipulated the victim so well that the victim will probably believe they can still 'make it right'. The victim will believe that they can still have some kind of friendship. The narce will play on this as much as they can. The victim's normal sense of fair play and concern will work in the narce's favor. The narce has no such feelings for the victim and will use their decency against them, every time.

"For example, during a divorce, the narce may say something like, "Come on, let's get this over with. I have an attorney who is a certified mediator. Let's meet at his/her office and settle this like adults." In truth, the last thing the narce wants is to 'settle this like adults.' The attorney is only interested in following the wishes of their narce client, who is paying them. The results of such a meeting should be obvious to us. It will not go well for the victim, who really wants a mature agreement. Instead, the victim will find themselves tricked and trapped by the attorney and the narce. They will find that the meeting did not occur on equal grounds.

"In every case, the narce will not only discard the victim but will make every attempt to ruin them. Chances are that the narce had carefully planned the breakup for a while. It is possible for any of the following conditions to exist: They had secret money; they had engaged in a smear campaign to ruin the victim's reputation; they had a place to go; they had carefully selected an attorney in advance; they may have even filed some of the paperwork and motions ahead of time, without the victim's knowledge. In short, the narce planned the discard to bleed the victim dry. They wanted to leave the victim penniless and friendless. Not only that, but they did it in a way that would make the narce smell like a rose.

"On the other hand, the victim will not understand this thinking. The narce will play on this as a weakness. The narce believes that there is great strength in cynicism and ego. In the narce's world, anyone who does have the strength to become a predator is now prey.

"We must remember that the *victim's natural compassion is not a weakness, it is a strength!* The narce sees their ability to discard and destroy people as a great strength because it enables them to get supplies. That is what the whole relationship, the whole discard, and the whole life of the narce are all about. It is about them getting supply. It could be money, cheap thrills, an ego boost, or anything else the narce craves.

"There are no limits to what the narce will do to look good and to destroy the victim during the discard. The narce will try to show the family and friends of the victim how wrong the victim was and why the narce *had* to leave the victim. They will declare that this is their liberation from the victim's many faults. The discard, just like the whole relationship, was all about appearances. The narce will claim their supply at the expense of the victim in any way they can.

"Remember that there are no boundaries, there are no limits to what the narce will do or claim. As painful as it is, when the discard occurs, the best and healthiest thing that the victim can do is to go completely *quiet, or in other words, make absolutely no contact with the* narce. It will not seem, intuitively, like a healthy thing to do. Going quiet would not be a healthy thing to do in a normal breakup, true, but this is not a normal breakup between two people of normal empathy. *This breakup involves a narce trying to crush someone.*

"In this case, all rules of normalcy go out the window. The victim is not dealing with a normal person. The rules of a healthy breakup do not apply because the narce does not understand what 'healthy' even looks like. They just want their supply! They want to be in the limelight, they want to look good no matter how bad they have been. They want to tear down the victim and make them appear to be a terrible human being.

"Even after the discard, the narce will continue to play cat-and-mouse with the victim. Any contact that the victim has with the narce will fit nicely into the narce's game. The narce will use any attention that they can get to their advantage. The narce would even go so far as to contact people that they mutually know to get information on the victim. Then the narce will carry things a step further to try and completely ruin the victim.

"To avoid further damage and ruination from the narce, the victim has to stop talking to them. If there are children involved, then the victim must arrange for communication to be done through the courts for visitation, to resolve custody issues, etc. The courts can provide options that will keep the narce and victim separated. During visitation, the victim must be careful what they reveal to the children. The victim must understand that the narce will badger the kids for information. Remember that there are no boundaries for the narce. They will use any means to communicate with or get information on the victim.

"Any information the narce gets, they will use it for their own purposes. The narce will try to derail any attempts the victim makes at success and at having a good life. Even though the narce discarded their partner, they will do all they can to keep tabs on the victim.

"Narces do this because they are terribly afraid of the victim. This is correct. You heard it right. The narce is afraid. It seems that the victim should be afraid because they are the prey. So why would the narce be afraid? Well, *the narce is afraid of the victim because the victim knows the truth about the narce!* Knowing that truth means the victim could expose the narce to the world. The narce cannot have that.

"Rather than risk exposure, the narce always rationalizes to the world what they did and why. Truth, in the mind of a narce, is subjective. For the narce, the truth will change at their convenience. The narce will distort the truth any way they have to. They will use a chameleon routine and look good no matter what they have done. The only hitch in this plan is that the victim knows and is telling the truth.

"The narce knows that eventually the truth will surface. This is the one thing fear. They fear the truth because it will expose the narce's weakness to the world. This would mar the narce's image and destroy their façade. The very thought of this is incredibly painful for the narce.

"This flaw in the narce's plan does not mean that if the victim tells the truth, all will be well. This does not mean that the victim will convince everyone of the truth. In fact, telling the truth about the narce will not work with a lot of people. The narce smear campaign has probably been in play from the beginning of the relationship. The narce has been planning the discard from the start. Smearing the victim way ahead of the discard prevents the narce from looking bad. The narce plans the discard and keeps it on the shelf for whenever they need it. Part of that plan is making the victims look so bad that no one will believe them when the truth is told.

"The victim, who is completely unaware of the smearing, is often shocked at how quickly people turn on them during the discard. Old friends will suddenly stop communicating. Family members may turn away. Gossip will flood the workplace. Any mutual acquaintances will hear all about how terrible the victim is. The narce will even involve total strangers in the smear if it is to their advantage.

"It may seem that the discard will destroy the victim. Make no mistake, it certainly can. The victim will have a sudden, forceful change in their life. They may lose money, friends, family, and means of support. The victim will see their whole life pulled out from under them. Indeed, the effects of an intentionally destroyed relationship will seem the same as a tornado or fire. The victim may feel shocked and lost. They will find themselves with part of their life suddenly ripped away, leaving them in a state of shock. It will seem hopeless to the victim, but there is hope if the victim learns to see the narce for what they are. The victim must then see that the breakup is not their fault.

"The truth is that the victim can build a whole new life if they learn and *accept* the truth. The victim can begin anew, once they break the trauma bond. The victim can learn to accept that people will side with the narce unjustly. Though it is painful, the victim can and must leave those people behind. The victim does not need the old friends any longer. The old friends have become toxic because they are on the side of the narce. The old friends have accepted the narce's twisted version of the truth. The old friends who have sided with the narce will always be the narce's flying monkeys. That makes them dangerous to the victim…Oh, I see you have a question, George."

"Frog… what is a 'flying monkey'?"

"Remember the movie *The Wizard of Oz*? Well, the Wicked Witch of the West used spies to gather information. The spies were these terrifying winged monkeys who would carry out missions for the witch. She would use them to seek out whatever tidbits she could gather on Dorothy and the others. The narce will do the same thing. They will use relatives, coworkers, mutual acquaintances, etc. to gather intelligence on what the victim might be doing."

"That is so unfair. All the victim wants to have their life back, to live as they see fit. They should be able to have old friends without worrying about what the narce will do."

"You are right. There is nothing fair about any of this. It is heartbreaking. Even though it is unfair, it cannot be changed. The victim must accept this. On the upside, accepting the truth will work in the victim's favor. These truths will liberate the victim from the flying monkeys, the narce's lies, and far-fetched stories.

"Once they understand and accept the truth, the victim must leave behind everything that they once shared with the narce. Commonalities such as mutual friends or even hanging out in the old haunts in the same town give the narce opportunity to learn of the victim. The less the narce knows, the better.

"When rebuilding their new life, the victim should not smear the narce, but they should tell the truth carefully to people who are important in their own life. This is done in case the narce happens to show up. And they will. The narce will show up at some wedding or funeral. They will show up at the grocery store if they and the victim live in the same town. The narce will show up because they cannot stand the fact that they have lost control of the victim. The narce will still try to find a way to smear the victim. The narce will try to regain control and ruin the freed victim any way they can.

"The narce wishes most of all that the freed victim would simply disappear from the face of the earth. They wish this because the victim knows the truth. The victim knows what really happened and the narce does not want to look bad. The truth is the narce's greatest enemy because the truth cannot be covered up forever. The freed victim can reveal the truth.

Frankly, the freed victim does not want the pain and drama of revealing the narce's true self to the world. All they want is the opportunity to rebuild their life. They want to live by the light they have inside. They want beauty and joy. That is all they want.

On the other hand, the narce believes that the victim is of the same character. They believe that the victim cannot wait to sully their reputation. They believe this, remember, because *they believe that everyone in the world is as nasty and vindictive as they themselves are.* This belief drives the narce's desire to control the victim, even after the discard.

"One more note: DO NOT underestimate the dangers that narce presents. These dangers are especially present in cases where the abuse is violent. There are cases where the narce has actually killed their victim to hide the truth.

"Before you jump to any conclusions, George, narces do not categorically try to kill their victims, but it does happen. The supply is usually what the narce is after, and that supply is gained most often by the narce wrecking the victim's plans for happiness. The narce will not stop trying to destroy the victim simply because they have discarded the victim. They think that the victim is inferior, the victim is a piece of property, and the victim is their tool to use at their pleasure. They will still try to use or hurt the victim in any way they can. We just had to mention the potential of murder because, sadly, it does exist."

When Frog stopped speaking, he looked me over carefully. He saw my tears as they flowed down my face. I could not believe what I was hearing. Again, I was overwhelmed and unsure of how to handle all of this. I still could not comprehend how people can be that way. It was very hard for me to take this all in. After a few minutes, I spoke. "Frog… Can I really do this? Can I really take all of this in and write a book about it?"

"George… that is entirely up to you. You have been called, as have many before you. But only you can decide to become chosen. If you really want to serve your fellow beings, you will find a way to handle this."

"Frog… I… " my voice trailed off and my head hung low. Frog let me be for a few minutes as the pond water gently lapped against the millstone. I wanted my fishing pole. Then after a few minutes, Frog spoke again.

"George, I think I have pushed you too hard in my eagerness to fulfill my mission. I think that you are the right one, but for now you need rest. I'll tell you what. Tomorrow, come back and bring your fishing pole. We will just sit here and you can quietly fish. How about that?"

"You'll let me keep the fish?" I asked as a small child would solicit their parent.

"If you catch anything of any size, yes, of course. I won't tell you what the fish are thinking, either. I promise to let you be."

"All right."

For the next two sessions, Frog watched me fish. He also watched my mind relax as I processed things. I fished and fished. I caught some little bluegills and released them. I finally caught a bass of some size and took him home for supper. It grilled up very nicely. The following day, I felt like myself again, and after work, I brought pens and paper instead of my fishing pole. Frog was elated. He said, "I thought we had lost you."

"No," I replied, "we have come too far and this thing has become way too intriguing for me to quit now."

"Good. Now, we need to talk about something that is quite treacherous and fearful. We have touched on it before, but will now cover it in depth. This is the narce technique we call the 'hoover'.

2 0

—

WATCH FOR THE HOOVER

As soon as I was ready to write, Frog continued with "A normal, healthy person does not want to see an important relationship end with absolutely no contact. Under normal circumstances, a healthy person will often want to have some kind of working friendship with their ex-, if the relationship is deep enough.

"The narce knows this and will try to do something to keep the victim in their circle, but only for more supply. The supply may not be enough to bother keeping the victim in a tight relationship, but any supply the victim can provide will feed the narce's false self. The supply-addicted narce is so desperate that they will take supplies in any way they can get them. Supply, emotionalism, drama, and control are literally like a drug to the narce they cannot live without it. The relationship was never about the other person.

"The method that the narce uses to fully or partially reclaim the victim is called 'hoovering'. The name comes from a brand of household vacuum cleaners, as you will see in your notes from our first couple of lessons. The narce wants to hoover the victim or suck them right back into their cycle of abuse. The narce will become friendly, or appear sorry that this or that did not work out. They will turn on the charm. They will use phrases that they know will control the victim. They will use the same emotional hot buttons

139

that they used during the relationship, etc. The narce does not want to lose supply. They do not want to lose control. So, they will do whatever they must to get the victim back into their circle.

"Sometimes, the narce will try to reclaim the victim completely, or sometimes they will bring the victim in just close enough to torment them. The narce believes that they are the 'ultimate person' and cannot stand the thought of the victim rejecting *them*. The narce does not want the victim to go until they say it is time. Control, remember, is the name of the game.

"Remember that the narce is no friend to anyone. They are no friend to the flying monkeys, they are no friend to the sources of supply they have around them. They are no friend to the victim, especially. The narce might use all kinds of friendly-looking motives to get next to the victim. They might just say "Congratulations on your promotion," or "I hear good things are happening for you," or maybe even "Have you seen that pair of shoes around your place, the ones I used to wear for formal occasions? Can I drop by and pick them up?" They may even say "Hey, how about a cup of coffee to work through some of our issues? I would like to be friends."

"The victim may be easily 'hoovered' by any of these phrases. All of these seem like reasonable and harmless requests. We must always remember that the narce is not a reasonable or harmless person. The best thing for the victim to do is hang up, block the narce's number and all social media they shared with the narce, move out of the area or whatever it takes to not allow any contact, no matter what their narce's reasons might be for keeping in touch.

"The narce could not care less about those shoes, they don't have any friendly feelings toward the victim's success, nor do they think they can work on 'issues'. In their mind, the narce has no issues. The victim was clearly the problem and owed them supply, so they would lie, manipulate, and do whatever they could to get that supply. It is a great thrill for the narce to be able to suck the victim back in after the discard. This is a very powerful tool narces use to keep the victim on their leash, to keep sucking supply out of them.

"The narce has no love for the victim; there are no tender feelings over fond memories and there is no joy in the heart of the narce. The only thing they have feelings for is their next supply fix. And if the victim is an empath who worked hard for the narce over years of a bad friendship or marriage, sucking the victim back in is like winning the Super Bowl!

"It is critical to remember that the narce is not harmless. There is no innocent cup of coffee. There is no innocent 'one dance'. These things are harmless with normal people, but there is nothing harmless about anything the narce does. Whatever they are trying to talk the victim into is for the narce's benefit. It is certain to cause harm to the victim.

"The healthiest thing that the victim can do is to take their life back. They can only do this one way. This one thing, done only one way, is also the perfect revenge against the narce."

"Frog," I interrupted, "revenge should not be the motive."

"You are absolutely right. Let me finish and you will see how this works. Narce victims are usually nice people who do not want revenge. They are usually empaths who are not capable of giving pain for pain. *Even if the victim happens to want revenge, they should not and must not seek it.* The narce is much better at revenge and the victim will likely lose. Remember how we discussed 'mirroring' the narce's behavior? How it never work? Well, seeking revenge is exactly that. Seeking revenge will reduce the victim to the narce's level.

"I am not talking about doing anything back to the narce, or somehow trying to affect their mutual social circle against the narce. What I am talking about is not an act of aggression. It is an act of passive resistance. This action does not feed the narce's supply by giving them battle. *Even so, the narce will unquestionably be driven up the wall by this one, simple thing.* That simple thing is *the victim going absolutely no contact!*

"This is what the victim must do if they are to move on and have any kind of a healthy life. Refer back to 'going dark'. That is what the victim must do. Now, if there are children involved or some other kind of circumstances that make going dark impossible, the next best thing to do is to 'gray rock'."

I stopped writing and looked up. "'Gray rock', Frog? What on earth is that?

21

GRAY ROCK METHOD

FROG SMILED AND SAID, "It is very simple. Sometimes, it may not be realistic for the victim to be completely out of touch. In some cases, there might be children involved that belong to both the narce and the victim. There might be a business arrangement that cannot be ended. They may own mutual property and still need to work things out. These are realities that may require occasional contact with the narce. The victim must remember that the narce is *not their friend and contact is not safe on any level for any amount of time.*

That being said, when contact is necessary between the narce and the victim, there is a method to keep the narce at arm's length. That method is called 'gray rocking'. This method is aptly named because there is nothing plainer or more uninteresting than a gray rock."

"Okay, now I am more puzzled," I said.

"I will clarify this immediately. Imagine, if you will, a hillside covered with rocks. Your eyes just naturally sweep over them and move on. Why? Because nothing is interesting there. The eyes see and the brain perceives that there is nothing there worth your time. No thrill, no threat, nothing of value. Time to move on.

"Now if there is a rock that is of a different color, or a different shape, then the eyes and mind will pay attention to find out why this is. We become curious and want to learn more. It is the same with people. Remember that the narce has spent a long time studying their liberated victim, we will call them a 'peer', for the lack of a better term, and will notice anything different. An apparent difference in the *peer* will make narce want to know what has changed.

"When they discover what is new, they will exploit that information in any way they can. The victim must avoid giving any information to the narce. Whenever they meet, the peer must keep the meetings as brief and uninteresting as they can. The must never say that they are happy or sad. They must not say that they have this or that. They must never reveal any plans, friendships, or jobs. They must not admit to having so much as a cold.

"Though it might be very hard to resist the urge to speak of improvements and better life conditions, it is critical to reveal nothing. If the narce wants to brag about themselves, the peer must cut the narce off, rudely if need be, and settle whatever business is at hand. They must avoid engaging the narce in any way other than quickly settling business. Get in. Get done. Get out. And leave nothing behind for the narce to use against them. Bear in mind that the narce can use anything at all.

"If the narce starts to press the peer for any information, the peer must simply leave the area. Get back to the business later. Leaving will show the narce that their once-victim will not put up with foolishness any longer. Gray rocking shows a non-response to the nonsense and it avoids the drama the narce is itching for. It denies them the information they want.

"Above all, the peer must remember that they have been humiliated by the narce before and lost their power to this person. This is all done by emotional and mental manipulation. This trap must be avoided at all costs. The way to avoid the trap is to avoid the narce. Engaging the narce in any way will allow them to hurt you again. The narce knows the peer to well for the peer to engage the narce successfully because the narce knows all of the peer's hot buttons.

"Gray rocking, when done properly, will allow the peer to keep a cool head. Emotion will be completely taken out of the situation. The victim will be able to escape a situation that the narce could normally escalate. Once the peer has gray rocked the narce long enough, they will effectively block the narce's supply. There is a pretty good chance that the narce will simply realize that the victim is not 'fun' anymore. This should keep the narce in line during any meetings.

"Take a moment and look back at the word 'fun'. That is right. The narce actually *enjoys* causing the victim to become upset. They love watching the victim struggle. They love sabotaging efforts at adult conversation. They love to see the frustration in the victim's eyes. All of this is because the narce is stunted in their emotional development and never understands how to grow into a kind, empathetic person. The gray rock method will help the victim take back control by using self-control. This puts the peer in the driver's seat, removing them completely from their former 'victim' status."

"Wow," said I. "This is pretty amazing, taking back one's life from the narce by simply controlling how you respond to them."

"Yes. It works very well. Naturally, going dark is the best thing to do, but when that is not possible, gray rocking is a close second," said Frog. Then he paused. "You know, George, we are very close to the end of our time together."

"I was starting to wonder about that."

"Your intuition is very strong. In fact, we have just one more topic to cover."

"I see," I said sadly.

"Now, old friend, there will be none of that. No sadness. I want you to take the next several days off of coming here. Don't come to the pond, don't fish here, don't come back to see me. I want you to just write. Go home and write. Put our story together into a book form, but don't print it just yet. Come back when you have done all that and we will cover the final topic that will surprise you."

"A surprise, huh?" my spirits began to improve. Something to look forward to.

"Yes. You may even want to debate the topic with me a bit. We shall see." Then with a twinkle in his eye, he plopped into the water and I was left alone on the old millstone. I sat still for a moment, then gathered my notes and took them home to start working.

Six days later, I had compiled the book.

22

FORGIVENESS

IT WAS a Friday night and I could not sleep well. Finally, the sun rose and I found my way, with pen and paper in hand, to the old grist wheel. Frog was floating quietly, softly croaking a joyful song as the sun rose. We watched the sunrise together, two old friends having a quiet moment. I was sad today, as though the dawn heralded the end of an era.

The light purple clouds stood still in the gentle breeze as the sky glowed a beautiful yellow-auburn. Then a vivid fluorescent orange ribbon began to trace the very edge of the great billowy clouds as they turned to violet, most stunningly. The backdrop to the clouds transformed into a shimmering canvas of bright yellow. Then, slowly, pale white sunbeams, reaching heavenward, contrasted the scene in spectacular beauty as the massive yellow orb we call the sun slowly crept over the horizon. This was a sunrise worth getting out of bed to witness.

After a little while, the sun broke through completely, dispersing the clouds and a glorious day began. Frog turned in the water and looked at me. His look was different, today. If a frog can look sorrowful, he did. I knew what was coming. It was the thought that disturbed me through the night. *Frog was going to leave me after this final lesson.* I knew it and he knew that I knew it.

"Yes, my friend, I am sorry to say that you are correct. I am leaving you after today."

"But… I feel that my journey has just begun. I guess I thought you would see me through to the end."

"I will be a support to you, but I cannot be with you in person. I have other matters to attend to. You have learned all you need to know but for this last lesson."

"I…" Tears filled my eyes. "I don't have the words, Frog. I just don't."

"Not for goodbye, no. But you do have all the words you need for your book. You have all the words you need to start your journey. Your words will also help you finish it. We will meet again, someday, before you know it. I promise. Now compose yourself, my friend. You must finish this lesson and the book, or else all of our time and effort will be wasted."

"Yes. Yes, I will finish. There. My eyes are dry. Now we may begin." I turned my mind from sentiment and to the business at hand. Time to learn. My pen was ready.

"It may seem strange to you, George, but you now need to write the word *forgiveness*."

"What? 'Forgiveness'? How could that be a topic after we wrote of such dreadful things?"

"I told you it would seem strange."

"Well, yes. I mean, let's be reasonable here. Why would anyone want to have their narce abuser back in their life? After all the abuse and the gray rocking and going dark…"

"This chapter is not about having the abuser back."

"But isn't that forgiveness? Taking someone back after you have been hurt? Isn't restoration a part of forgiveness?"

"Restoration is part of forgiveness, yes."

"Then does that not mean that the relationship is to be restored?"

"If both parties can do so in a healthy way, then yes."

"But what if the narce is not healthy?"

"Then the narce cannot be invited back. It would be destructive to do so. The narce would believe that if they treated the freed victim, let us call them the 'peer', like this and such, but was still allowed back, then peer must have been okay with it."

"Then why forgive?"

"Because it is vital to the health and well-being of the peer."

"But does that not mean to invite the toxic narce back?" I was becoming confused and frustrated. It seemed like Frog was talking in circles.

"No. *In fact, the peer must not invite the toxic narce back.*"

"So… forgiveness can still happen even if the narce is not brought back."

"Precisely. The peer must forgive the narce, but not have the narce back. The narce will only do more damage upon their return if they are truly a narce."

"So, how does one know?"

"There is a difference between one being a little selfish and being a narce. For instance, maybe my life partner says I spend too much time on a new lily pad, and I am actually doing so because I am feeling selfish. That lily pad makes me look really cool.

"Then maybe I really want other things that we cannot afford. I start over-spending, getting more cool stuff, and neglecting my partner. My partner confronts me on it, and we figure a way through, with mutual understanding. We discover that I am willing to not have this or that comfort for the sake of the financial situation. We agree that my partner will allow reasonable concessions and I give up unreasonable demands. Our relationship stays intact. That initial selfishness does not make me a narce."

"What would make you a narce then?"

"If I demanded that you provide me 'cool' things, such as needlessly expensive clothes or entertainment devices. Then, I would expect you to praise me for buying them. Then if you didn't like it, I tell everyone around us how mean you are to me. I would say you are lazy and you refuse to provide because you don't care about my needs.

"Feeling entitled to more than our income can provide, I would open a secret credit account. I may even work a secret job to buy the things I want while basic life needs such as rent and groceries are not being met. Then, if you find out about it and confront me over it, I will tell you that you have no right to do so. After all, if you provided for me properly in the first place, I would not have to sneak around. You made me sneak around because if I didn't I would not ever have these things I need."

"Ah. Yes. Big difference. The spendthrift could be reasoned with, but narce will demand and blame shift. It seems that the demands and blame shifting would apply to about every situation in which the narce would find themselves."

"There is hope for you yet, George," Frog laughed. "I had hoped you would realize that there is a difference between human fault and narcissism. You have done well, and I am glad you have arrived at this understanding before our final meeting ended."

"Thank you, Frog. Now what about forgiveness?"

"Yes. Forgiveness is not about restoring an unrepentant, toxic person to your life."

"Can the narce ever change?"

"Perhaps, but it would be very rare for any lasting changes to occur. They may pretend for a while just to impress the peer, but they will revert to old ways once they have their victim back. It would be very rare for a true narce to make lasting changes."

"Um…" I looked through my notes. "The narce would commit hoovering. Their good behavior would leave bread crumbs. This could create Stockholm syndrome on the part of the victim… ?"

"Precisely! Very impressive, young one. I expected you to miss the Stockholm's part, and instead, you nailed it! Now, and this is very important, remember that the things we are sharing here are only the beginning of the journey. For a person to fully understand narcissism and its effects, they must study and learn from other sources as well. Some people might read your book who will realize that they have been harmed by a narce.

"People who realize they have been hurt deeply should consider getting professional help along with their studying. People will often need help to pass through the trauma and pain they will suffer while going through all of this. The trauma bond is not an easy thing to break. The victim will likely feel lost and alone during this process. We want a positive ending for the victim, not a tragic conclusion to a heartbreaking story."

"I understand that the peer must forgive the narce for their own health. Even so, I feel as though the narce is getting away with an awful lot. I don't believe that the victim should be punished, no. But seems to be unjust, somehow, that the narce lives along contentedly as they manipulate their victims, maybe even ruining their lives. Then they kick these hurt people aside and move on to new victims. Narces get to be happy with their lives, even as they leave destruction in their wake."

"*Happy,* you say? Oh, my, my, my dear man! We missed something along the way," Frog chuckled, seemingly surprised.

"What do you mean?" I asked, curiously. "I thought we covered it all."

"Maybe we did not cover this point as thoroughly as we should have. We did discuss it briefly, but it seems we still have just one lesson left."

2 3

THE NARCE'S HIDDEN PAIN

I SETTLED back on the grist wheel and waited for Frog to gather his thoughts. Then he began. "It is easy, in this study of the harm narces do, to skip over one very critical point. I sometimes think that we should not even care about this. Despite our initial misgivings, it is critical to remember that *special something* which motivates the narce to constant supply."

"Well, yes. We have covered the idea that supply is an addiction."

"Correct. It is an addiction. Do you know why?"

"Um… no, not unless… Well… it seems that the narce sees this as happiness…?"

"Ah, yes. Now I see where we missed the point. When we were talking about supply, we glossed over something very important. Why does the narce crave supply? Why do they want support, attention, praise, and glory?"

"Because… they crave it. We've been over that. What am I missing?"

"Why do they crave it?"

I read back through my notes and discovered that the narce was taught by some circumstance in life that they must be in control at all times. "They crave it because control is the thing they need."

"Yes. Now answer the question: Why does a drug addict need their fix?" asked Frog.

"They need that fix because they are hurting without it. We talked about that in the 'social abuse' section."

"Uh-huh… now think that over a minute."

"Just like a drug addict, narces are hurting without their fix. For the narce, supply is their narcotic. Without it they have pain."

"Yes. You just hit the nail on the head. Just stop thinking about it in terms of physical health. Forget the physical pain of the addict, the muscular cramping, the vomiting, nausea, and headaches. Think of it in terms of a narce's emotional state."

"The narce's emotional state? Well, let's see… They are *emotionally* hurting. So, the fix of supply is going to numb their emotional pain, but only temporarily. That is why they need more."

"Yes. Why did they start on the road to a supply addiction?"

"To cover pain… Oh! Yes. I see now. At some time in life, the narce suffered some kind of pain, trauma, or scarring that they simply cannot face. Am I correct?"

"Yes. Keep going."

"Okay. The narce has some difficulty that they must keep covered up. Their pride won't allow them to be vulnerable. They cannot face the pain of their weakness, that is, their imperfection. The have developed the idea that somehow, they must cover up their pain by punishing and controlling other people. This gives them the need to believe that they are the superior specimen of humanity. They are more loving, beautiful, stronger, etc. than any other person. When something comes up that reveals their weakness, it reminds the narce that they are not the ultimate specimen. They cannot stand that."

"What do we call that, then?"

"Narcissistic injury. I remember the term. Does the narce tell their followers about it?"

"No, only the narce knows about the injury. They will not admit to the pain, because that would expose a weakness. They cannot bring themselves to admit weakness. Having weaknesses would give others an advantage over them. The narce believes the rest of the world to be the same as they, so the world must be out to take advantage."

"That sounds like a terrible way to live."

"It is."

"Without trust, can the narce ever know love? Or is supply their only love?"

"No, they never know love because that requires vulnerability. Supply, as their addictive drug of choice, is all they know or care about."

"I see. Should feel sorry for them?"

"That is up to you. I know I do. Now, in that sorrow, I also realize that I might want to fix them."

"We talked about that. I remember how we said that the narce will use an empath's desire to help against them."

"Yes. That is why the narce must be avoided. Not only that, but the narce will never want the empath around unless the empath is their victim. They will never want the empath near them as a peer. They know that the empath knows their weakness and feels their pain. The narce does not want to have anyone around them who knows the truth. The truth is too painful for them to face and they know that the empath brings them face-to-face with their flaws."

"My guess, then, is that the narce will do all they can discredit the empath. They will completely reject and destroy them if possible."

"That is correct."

"All narces live with this pain all the time. They have no satisfaction or build any real character. They live a hollow existence, trying only to avoid pain."

"Yes."

"Then I choose to not envy the narce. I choose to avoid them, no matter what successes they may have in their lives."

"You will need to emphasize to your readers that they cannot 'fix' the narce. They must not 'pity' the narce. They must not associate with the narce unless it is absolutely necessary and then do so on minimal, gray rock terms. Never appear interested in them or what they do. Don't do anything around them to stand out, either. Keep them guessing and never tell them anything. Soon, they will leave you alone. They may try to discredit you behind your back. Don't let them bother you. Just be important to people who support you and let the rest go."

"I will try to remind them of that, Frog."

I finished writing my final notes. I could think of nothing else that I needed to say, do or ask. I just looked at Frog and dreaded what he was about to tell me. He said exactly what I thought he would.

"Now, George… my friend and fellow servant… It is my time. I have to go now. You have all that you need to get started on this project of yours."

"Yes, publishing the book." I paused and began choking back tears. "How will I do it without you?"

"You don't need me anymore, George. Publishers will have an interest in your book. Just remember to add a glossary to the end of the book so people can have a decent start on narce vocabulary. I must go, now."

"I know… so, Frog… will I see you again?"

"Perhaps in your dreams. Or perhaps at another pond. Good-bye, my good friend."

As soon as Frog bade farewell, I developed tunnel vision. Things became fuzzy and I felt like I was in an echo chamber. Frog, the pond, all of it just faded away. Then, all at once, my eyes closed and all went black. I opened my eyes again. I shook my head, opened my eyes and they slowly focused. I found myself to be at home, in bed. I realized that Old Man Bryant's pond was forty-three years past and seventeen hundred miles away. I rolled out of bed, grabbed one of my legal pads, and started writing before I lost the details of the dream.

Perhaps I had dreamed a dream no mortal dared to dream before, I thought.

I began writing furiously, but then noticed something…There was a small *lily pad* sitting on my desk, with a few drops of pond water splashed around. Beside these were some legal pads full of my handwriting, and several pens… Yellow sparks were dancing in the room, vanishing as quickly as I discerned them.

The End

Or Perhaps this is Your New Beginning!

GLOSSARY

WITH AUTHOR'S NOTES AND EXPLANATIONS

Abuse: Any damaging behavior to anyone which involves injury to the victim in any way (physically, mentally, socially, financially, etc.) is abuse. The narce will treat those closest to them the worst. When they discard their victim, they will do all they can to destroy that person, as a person.

Attention: The narce craves attention because to them, being overlooked, ignored, and not being made the constant center of attention is like suffocating them. They must have attention. They crave attention. If they don't get that attention, they will find a way to get it or someone will pay. Their behavior can be pushy, rude, or completely outlandish.

Blame Shifting: The narce will not accept responsibility for any wrongdoing. They will blame others for their own behavior. "You made me mad" is a throw-away phrase someone uses when they are upset by another person's actions, but most people don't mean it literally. What they really mean is "I have become upset by what you have done." In the narce's case, though, they are shifting the blame for their anger onto someone else. They will also shift responsibility for their behavior onto another person. Examples: A narce may shift their overspending behavior onto the victim with the idea the narce is not overspending. They will say they are just seeing to their own "needs" that the victim cannot provide. *If the victim made more money, there would be no* *financial problems.* The narce will blame the partner for a failure in the relationship that "makes the *narce* cheat" because their "needs are not being met" in the relationship. *If the partner had not gained weight, if the partner was more considerate, if the partner did this or that differently, then then* narce *would not feel the need to cheat.* Rarely will the narce accept responsibility for any failure in the home, family, business, or relationship. When they say that they do, it is usually to impress someone.

Boundaries: The narce will always keep their guard up to prevent the victim from entering their world and learning about them, lest the victim should uncover the narce's weaknesses. They don't want to give the victim anything they could use against the narce later. At the same time, the narce will not allow the victim to have any boundaries. The narce will insist on learning all about the victim. The narce will always walk all over the victim's rights to be who they are. They will criticize and condemn anything that the victim does. They will criticize the way the victim drives, the way they talk or eat, the movies they watch and anything about them in much more intense and unhealthy ways than a person should.

Brain Damage: Prolonged abuse of any kind causes actual physical, chemical and neurological changes in the brain. The changes take place because of the high level of stimulation under which the victim of a narce abuser lives. This state of overstimulation causes some parts of the brain to grow and others to shrink. This very real form of injury occurs because the victim is constantly struggling to survive the emotional conflicts, the highs, the lows, the constant arguing, financial damage, surprises, and chaos that the narce brings to the table. This is why the survivor of narce abuse needs help and a strong support network. This is why the survivor who leaves the narce needs to recognize that (1) they are damaged, (2) the fault is not theirs, and (3) there is *hope!*

Brain Fog: This is a very real confusion that keeps the victim from thinking clearly. The victim's head gets all "foggy", or their mind is unclear, and they have difficulty discerning between what is correct and incorrect *(Does 2+2=4 or not?).* Brain fog can affect the victim's ability to discern between morally right and wrong. This imbalance in thinking is intentionally created by the narce. It is not imaginary; it is very real and can cause some serious issues for the victim. The fog comes from the narce causing blurred boundaries, negativity, and self-doubt in the victim.

Brainwashing: This is a term that is loosely thrown around by the unknowing. Sometimes, it is confused with "manipulation". A person who has been manipulated may change their actions and thinking for a time but will come back to their own true self. However, a person who has been brainwashed, truly brainwashed, is a terrible thing to behold. It is difficult to reclaim a brainwashed person, and we have seen such people emerge from religious cults and cults of personality with serious mental issues. A brainwashed person is difficult to reclaim and will need a lot of therapeutic treatment to get over the changes that were forced upon them by the narce and their followers. Know that every narce is out to at least manipulate, and ultimately brainwash, if possible, anyone they encounter.

Bread Crumbs: Little fragments of favor, kindness, or promises given to keep the victim hopeful that the relationship will change, even though it will not. When the narce sees that the victim is starting to wonder about the validity of the relationship, they will throw the victim a crumb of happiness and hope here and there. It will be just enough to keep the victim interested and hopeful that the relationship will work out. As soon as the victim is hopeful, the narce will return to the old ways and dash those hopes. More bread crumbs will appear later to create more false hope in a never-ending cycle. Bread crumbs are part of the "hoovering" process, as listed below.

Bully: The narce is the ultimate epitome of "the bully". Narces are mean and will get their way by force. They do not care what form that force takes. They do not care how much they must lie, manipulate, cheat, or steal. They have no problem at all doing whatever they must to get their supply. Just like a bully, they will take up with others and form a gang that will constantly seek to destroy the victim. The gang, led by the narce, consists of flying monkeys and people who have otherwise been manipulated to side with the narce. The narce has no boundaries and does not care about "fairness". The narce will take revenge on the victim for daring to defy them, particularly if the victim starts achieving things without the narce's consent. Bullying is any action that takes control away from the victim or causes them harm in any form. Social, mental, financial, physical, or any abuse in any form is bullying.

Chameleon: The narce, because they are disingenuous, can easily slip into different situations and can change the mask of their personality at the drop of a hat. The "personality" and motives of the narce never change. They change their appearance only. They can sound loving, joyful, and friendly to someone they are trying to impress. In fact, they can change their tune to impress anyone. If they need to become crude of speech, they can do that. If they need to express understanding for points of view they secretly hate, the narce will do that. The narce is capable of changing their tune to anything the situation calls for to impress and influence the person or group they are in front of at the time. The mask, though, may slip from time to time and the perceptive potential victim will notice this and avoid further dealings with the narce.

Change: Healthy people see the need to change and grow. The narce does not. The narce believes themselves to be perfect just the way they are. Do not expect the narce to change for long, even if they put on the appearance of change. They will do so as part of hoovering, as part of creating false hope. The victim, though, may change and grow beyond the narce. In this thought, there is hope.

Chaos: The narce will create as much chaos as they can in any relationship. They thrive on chaos. They want their needs to be catered to and then they will block the efforts of their victim to fulfill those needs. This creates confusion and negative energy in the victim, which is precisely what the narce wants. They love to create as much chaos as they can and will always choose the most dramatic path they can in so doing.

Charisma: Many narces are charismatic, bubbly people. They are always nice, complimentary, socially graceful, and so on to new people. Narces often have many qualities that people admire. They will use those qualities to get control of others and collect supplies from them. The narce will appear so wonderful that people in their family, social, and religious circles will not believe the narce is an abuser. A notorious example of charismatic influence would be Ted Bundy, the serial killer who was executed by an electric chair in 1989. Many in his social/religious circle could not believe that the man was a serial killer. Some church people and their children even sent him letters of love and support in jail, firmly believing in his innocence.

Circular Arguments: These "conversions" as the narce will call them, are nothing more than no-win arguments. For example:

Narce: "You don't make enough money."

Victim: "We have the money for what we need."

Narce: "Our needs are not met."

Victim: "Stop squandering the money on things for you."

Narce: "I am meeting my needs."

Victim: "We could both meet our actual needs with what we have."

Narce: "We don't have enough money. If we did, my needs and our needs would both be met."

Victim: "Stop spending so much on yourself."

Narce: "If you made enough money, my needs would be filled and we would not be having this conversation."

Etc., Etc.

Co-dependent: The narce is very codependent. *Their unhappiness or their anger is dependent upon something the victim did or did not do.* Narces make their happiness and satisfaction dependent on the victim's actions. Their unhappiness and dissatisfaction is always someone else's fault. They will never take responsibility for their own moods and emotional states. They will blame the victim for circumstances that the victim did not create. Usually, the narce creates the problem and shifts the blame to the victim.

Competition: The narce will always compete with others, even in the smallest, pettiest things. They will always try to outdo the victim in particular because they must know that they are better than the victim. It could be something as simple as table manners or the way the victim ties their shoes. The narce has to compete in every little thing, on every little level because they need to feel like a winner. The victim will not even realize they are involved in a competition. The narce will gloat at every perceived "win" and they will receive a narcissistic injury at every "loss". The victim will pay for that injury in some subtle way without even realizing they caused the injury. The most important thing to remember is that *only the narce knows about the competition, its rules and the win/loss tally.*

Covert Narcissist: This is a type of narce that will keep their tendencies under wraps and try to pretend that they are not selfish. The covert narce will passively abuse the victim. If the victim mentions it, the narce will throw a fit and tell the victim how selfish they are. An example of this might be the narce ignoring basic hygiene and telling the victim they should love them anyway, no matter how they appear or even how they smell. After the confrontation is over, a covert narce would perhaps clean up and appear normal to others, then complain against their victim. This is to make the victim look crazy or unreasonable. This is a gaslighting approach and covert narces are masters of gaslighting.

Crack the Door: This occurs when the former victim, or "peer" allows the narce ANY room in the new life that they are creating post-discard or after realizing they must leave the relationship. The peer must understand that the narce cannot tolerate the fact that the victim has become a peer. The narce needs the supply of the former victim and will do everything it can to reclaim that supply. They will use social media that is open to them, they will use family and friends to check up on their peers, and they may leave things with their peers to make an excuse to drop by. So much as a cup of coffee with the narce is leaving an opening for the narce to slowly, insidiously regain control. The peer must close the door completely and go dark.

Dark (Also see 'No Contact'): Despite the obviously negative connotation of the word 'dark', this is not something that the narce does to the victim. Going 'dark' is the only way to defeat the narce. *The victim must keep the narce out of their life and away from them no matter how many friends and family members they lose to the narce.* Remember: *Do not get drawn into the* *narce competition and there is no "getting even. The only "revenge" the victim gets is to go dark and leave the narce out in the cold for the rest of their lives. The narce absolutely cannot stand that their victim is living without them, and thriving. This means that the victim has become a "peer" (see below.) It is a sweet irony that the safest thing the peer can do is also the one thing that will drive the narce completely nuts. The narce will pretend that it does not matter, but they deeply miss the supply that was unique to that former victim.*

Deflecting: This occurs when a narce tells the victim that they are the problem. The abusive narce will say that the victim is the one abusing them. The spendthrift narce will blame the victim for their financial troubles. The narce will also deflect their faults onto the victim directly as in saying "Oh, you think you are so perfect" or "You just always have to run everything, don't you?" when in fact, the narce is the self-proclaimed perfect one who must run everything. This is a common tactic the narce use when they are having "conversations" with their victim.

Devaluing Stages: Degrading, demeaning, humiliating, shaming and more are all part of the devaluing stages. The narce will always try to make the victim feel as though they are less than the narce is, particularly in front of others. It could be at a family gathering, at dinner with friends, or in any group setting. It goes even further than that, though. They will keep degrading and devaluing the victim in private too, causing the victim to doubt themselves. They do this to keep the victim off balance, to keep the victim in a cycle of living to please their abuser. This is at the heart of narce abuse. Their devaluing of others ruins lives and hurts people terribly. Then comes the 'discard'.

Discard: This is the inevitable result of a narce relationship, whether it is romantic, friendly, or of professional interest. The narce will eventually "discard" anyone who no longer provides a supply, plain and simple. The victim will simply be cast aside. It will not make sense, it will not be logical, it will be perplexing and the narce will always see the destruction of the relationship as the victim's fault. The discard is terribly painful because of the cold finality of it. If there are mutual children involved, the narce will do all they can to take them. The narce will try to erase the victim from the face of the earth. At the same time, they will also try to keep the victim on the hook to further torment them. The narce will continue devaluing the victim. They will try to keep the victim in a state of misery. The narce may even torment the victim by showing off "how wonderful" they are doing with the victim out of their life. Even the smallest degree of the victim's attention after the discard is a source of narce supply.

Disloyalty: The narce will never be loyal to the supply, the victim, or to anyone. The narce is not out for lasting love or relationships. They are only out to get supply and will string the victim along for months, years, or decades. During that entire time, the narce is talking about the victim. They tell others how their partner is nothing without them. They also magnify the faults, or supposed faults, of the victim. The victim is not even aware this is happening because they believe in the mask that the narce uses when the victim is around. The things the narce says to others are always kept secret from the victim.

Domestic Abuse: The narce will always be abusive in the home. If anyone notices trouble in the home, the narce will never admit fault. The narce will always blame other people for causing the chaos. No one at home is free from their wrath. The narce will abuse the victim and anyone who dares to stand up for the victim. The narce always has their own agenda ahead of the family/household and their happiness. Even children have no boundaries. The narce will not hesitate to abuse the children emotionally, hoover them and re-earn their trust. They will condemn the other parent of the children for this or that. The narce will pressure the kids to cast the other parent aside. Narce abuse may also become physical.

Egotism: Everything is about the narce. All things must be to their standard. All people must believe their way, behave their way, speak their way, and so on. It is a gross understatement to call a narce a mere egotist. It is important to understand that while all narces are egotists, not all egotists are narces. A person may be irritatingly egotistical about certain abilities, but a true narce is a whole different breed of human. The true narce believes that they are the absolute best and final example of what a human being should be. They will despise anyone who does not support that illusion in all times and places. An egotist is an annoyance, but a true narce is a destroyer who lacks any compassion or empathy for anyone else.

Empath: An empath is a person who genuinely senses and always considers the feelings of others. It the empath is not careful, they can easily become trapped in a people-pleasing mode. Narces always seek empaths because they are natural givers and servants while the narce is a natural taker who must be served. The empath is content to give, the narce is content to take. This works well while the narce is in the love bombing or "fun" mode of the relationship. Then after the fun ends for the narce, the empath begins to weaken. They feel terrible as the narce slowly devalues them and takes everything.

Empathy: The human quality that people have that allows them to put on the other guy's shoes and try to understand how they may feel. Empathy causes us to say "My heart goes out to you," or "I am trying to understand how that must feel." Know this about the narce: *They have no empathy.* The narce will play at having empathy and will try to appear as though they have understanding. Know that this is just one of the many masks and disguises that the narce uses to get their way.

Energy: The narce intentionally creates negative energy. They do this to drain and weaken their victim. Circular arguments, negative comments, gossip, and other poor behavior drain a normal, empathic person. The narce is self-centered and only out to gain their supply. This lifestyle will drain the partner of the narce, who is a victim, of their life force. The narce creates this negativity and weakness intentionally because they actually thrive on it.

Entitlement: The narce believes they are entitled to treat anyone anyway they like. They think that should be catered to. They believe that they are supposed to be the center of attention. They believe that all people should simply do as they say. No one should question them, or ever do anything else the narce does not like. They see people as a source of supply, whatever that may be, to sustain the narce. Anyone who does not feed into the narce's ideals will soon be dismissed from the narce's circle. Only "useful" people are allowed to remain there.

Ether: When we refer to "the ether", it is a nod to a colorless liquid whose fumes will cause someone to sleep if they are exposed to it. This simple term describes the state of the manipulated mind. The narce abuses their victim with gaslighting, humiliation, sabotage, isolation, etc. to the point that the victim does not even really know who they are anymore. It is almost as though some parts of the victim's personality have been put to sleep. The victim changes and often becomes something that their family and old friends no longer recognize. This is because the narce is twisting the victim into what they want the victim to become: *A weakened, subservient mess.* It all starts with the mind-numbing manipulation.

Expiration Expectation: The narce knows that no one will live forever. They know that no one will put up with their abuse forever. The narce knows that sooner or later, all relationships must come to an end. They are not in a relationship for the long game, for commitment, or for love. Even business partnerships and friendships must end for them because the victims will eventually discover what the narce really wants. So, the narce will cultivate multiple sources of supply. As soon as one source of supply drops off the radar, the narce already has another lined up to take their place.

Fake Repentance: This is just another way of describing the narce's hoovering, future faking, and other forms of manipulation to convince the victim that they have changed. "Repentance" is commonly used as a religious term, but it simply means that a person has changed for the better after harming. That being said, fake repentance is a very common narce method in religious circles. The narce wants to look good in the religious community. They revel in the supply that the community offers. Looking good to the religious community can be a huge narce supply because they can still be a jerk and do so in the name of God. The narce as a parent or spouse may be abusive, but still, look good to their religious community. The narce may even win the religious community's full support, all the while blaming the victim.

False Hope: This term means exactly what the words imply. It is a tool used by the narce to lead the victim on and on. The whole time the victim is chasing hope for the relationship that simply does not exist. The narce will do things like show kindness, or project wonderful ideas about what the future will be like. This will give the victim hope for the relationship. That hope is completely false. That hope does not exist. False hope is used by the narce to get the victim back under control when the victim is starting to distance themselves from the narce.

False Self: The narce does not have a realistic idea of who they are. For some not yet fully understood reason, whether from being abused or unreasonably built up as a child, the narce always believes themselves to be superior. The reality-based person knows that they may be superior in *some* ways to other people, by gifts, talents, learning, or some other factors. But that person also knows that others are superior to them in some ways, too. People, generally, accept that they have limitations and weaknesses, but the narce will not ever admit this. The narce has constructed a false self that must never be challenged or overthrown. If the false self is exposed, the narce will experience great emotional pain when they find out that they are not better than all others in all things. They will avoid that pain at all costs.

Far-Fetched Stories: The narce will always interpret and paint the victim in the worst possible light to everyone they meet. Remember that the narce always has to be the hero. They must be the knight in shining armor. They must be victims of the story that overcame the odds and got away from the terrible monster who was draining the life out of them. The narce will say whatever they have to say to get sympathy and a new supply. The victim will be demonized to total strangers who meet the narce. People who don't even know the victim will be convinced the victim is of low character and possibly even a criminal of some kind.

Flying Monkeys: Remember the Wicked Witch of the West from *The Wizard of Oz?* Remember her little messengers, those horrid, winged monkeys that would do her bidding? Well, every narce has several of these little messengers that come around to find out information on the victim. The narce has convinced these messengers that the victim is somehow flawed or even a bad, bad person. Flying monkeys can be anyone, especially people who the narce and victim mutually know. The narce has no boundaries and will even turn the victim's own family against them. Remember, too, that the narce is turning to new sources of supply and will not hesitate to send strangers around to check up on the victim. If you are in the middle of narce breakup, this is a good time to "gray rock" with anyone who seems to be asking strange or probing questions. Your instincts absolutely will not lie to you. If someone seems "off", they are likely working with the narce.

Forgiveness, Narcissistic: The victim must remember that there are two kinds of forgiveness. There is normal healthy forgiveness where one no longer holds the other accountable. Then there is the narce's forgiveness which means that they will allow the victim the good grace of remaining in an assigned role in the narce's life. The narce actually believes that the victim cannot live without them, and is waiting with opens arms for the victim to return to some specific assignment in the narce's life. The narce hopes the victim will try to win back the narce's affection, allowing the narce to torment them some more. As long as the victim plays the assigned role granted by the narce, the victim will be permitted to remain in the circle.

Forgiveness, Victim's: It will be hard, but the victim must learn to forgive the narce. When the victim finally forgives, they will be released from the narce. Otherwise, without forgiveness, the victim will be tied to the narce, hating them. The narce wants the victim to hate them. The *hateful* victim will forever ruminate about the narce. This rumination gives the narce a place in the victim's life, by default. The narce wants the victim to think about them always, even if it is hateful. The frustration of the victim is sweet nectar to the narce. Forgiveness is a release, a wonderful peace for the victim, and it will be a sense of relief and freedom that they have not known for a long time, if ever. Remember that the narce wants the victim to be in their clutches. The victim should claim their freedom by forgiveness.

CRITICAL NOTE: Healthy forgiveness does not include bringing the toxic narce back into the victim's life. Such would be very destructive for the victim. Forgiveness as spoken here is the final release that will free the victim who is under no obligation to return to the narce for more abuse. It is important to realize that the victim does not have to confront the narce, or contact the narce in any way as part of forgiveness. They do not need to tell the narce at all, not even by a third party, that they, the victim have forgiven them.

Simply put, "Go dark and forgive. Then remain dark." The narce does not need to know of the forgiveness. Let it all go!

Future Faking: This is another tactic that the narce uses to keep the victim under control. Future faking involves the narce creating this utopic fantasy of how wonderful everything will be between you and them. Future faking is a huge part of love bombing, particularly effective in romantic relationships. This is also a big part of what the narce may do to hoover the victim. The narce will make promises they cannot keep. The impossibility does not matter because even if they could, they would not keep the promises, anyway. They will try to make the picture of their fake future together seem irresistible to the victim.

Gaslight: This is about the narce trying to keep the victim confused. For example, they will say "Get a pound of cheddar cheese at the store." The victim knows what they said. They bring it home and they will say something like "I told you Swiss cheese! You know I can't make this recipe without Swiss! Cheddar? Don't be ridiculous. You know better." These are intentional things that the narce does to make the victim think they are mistaken about what they hear, see, feel, believe, and think. This, over time, will eventually cause the victim to stop believing in their own perceptions. Self-doubt keeps the victim vulnerable, which is precisely where the narc wants the victim to be. The narce wants the victim to trust the narce's word more than they trust themselves.

Ghosting: A form of abuse where the narce acts as though the victim is not even there. They will treat the victim as though they do not, and did not ever really matter. For instance, a newly married couple may break up by the narce taking stuff from the home and maybe or maybe not leaving a note. The breakup will be sudden, without real explanation, and terribly final. The narce may even see the victim later just by chance, say at the grocery store, and will walk by them without acknowledging their existence. If they speak to the victim at all, it will only have the purpose of tormenting the victim further because it will be a casual nod or greeting, as though the marriage or relationship meant nothing. For indeed, to the narce, it did mean nothing.

Gray Rock: Gray-rocking is a term that describes going completely "bland" around the narce. It is a form of self-defense that is highly effective. To gray-rock is to simply not show the narce how well you are doing. Do not tell them about the business you started, the new book you wrote, new friends you've made, and especially not a new love interest. This technique is very important because the narce will always want to know how the victim is doing. The victim must do this so that the narce does not know how well they are or how much they are hurting. It is important to go no-contact with the narce, but when there are children, or if you live in the same town and cannot move, or have other situations make no-contact impossible, gray-rocking is a close second. When the victim gray rocks, the narce gets no supply, no argument, no drama, and no fun. The narce will simply leave the victim alone because they get nothing from them.

Happiness: A state of being that the narce has only on occasion. The narce will have what they believe to be happiness only for as long as they have their "supply". That supply is always at the expense of another person. The narce depends on others to "make them happy" and actually holds people responsible for keeping them in that state of supply. The thing that they call "happiness" never lasts for long, and when the narce is no longer happy, victims pay until the narce is given more supply. Healthy people, on the other hand, enjoy levels of happiness and satisfaction in their lives that the narce will never know.

Hoover: This is a brand of vacuum cleaner and has nothing to do with Herbert Hoover, the 31st President of the United States. When in the act of "hoovering", the narce will do something to drive you away and then will make all kinds of flattering attempts to re-attract you, to suck you back in. The narce will never want to be "rid" of you, even after they discard you. They will want to find some way to bring you back to them so that they may punish you more. There are usually several hoovers during the relationship. It is a never-ending cycle of punishing and then drawing the victim back in. They will likely create false hope and/or use fake repentance as part of this process.

Identity Crisis: The victim of narce abuse will always go through an identity crisis. This is because the narce has manipulated and molded the victim for so long that they no longer know who they truly are. The victim has been told they are not good enough. They have been told that their talents mean nothing. They have been exposed to devaluation and degradation for so long that they have likely lost themselves along the way. Being so removed from the talented, kind, light-filled person that they truly are, the victim no longer has an accurate self-image. Add into this complicated mix the strong likelihood that the victim is not only empathic but may have grown up abused and you have the perfect storm. That is why the narce will try to find an empath with weak boundaries from an abusive home.

Isolation: Remember that it is the narce's goal to control others. They know that people who are alone are easier to manipulate and easier to control. With that in mind, they never hesitate to isolate the victim. The narce is going to always remove family, friends, and other social supporters from the life of the victim. The only people permitted to remain in the narce's circle are under the narce's influence. This further isolates the victim because the narce now has a gang to work against the victim.

Juvenile Thinking: The narce will have a very underdeveloped style and type of thinking. They believe that they are the center of the universe. The emotional development of the narce never matured beyond their mid to late teen years. The narce never thinks beyond those years. They are stuck in that stage of human development. When someone disagrees with them, they will get back at that person, much like a mean "jock" or "cheerleader" in one of those adolescent 'coming of age' movies. The narce believes that anyone who steps on their "territory", which is their circle of victims and supporters, is their *enemy*. Remember that the narce believes the world is their exclusive territory. They think that they should decide who has what, who should be with whom, etc. It is important to note the narce will get worse with age.

Lies: The victim must be ready to endure lies from the narce, particularly when the victim is trying to escape the narce. This goes right along with the smear campaign and the far-fetched stories. Remember that the narce has no boundaries and is stunted in their emotional growth. The narce remains in a childish, selfish state and will have no qualms at all about lying to anyone who will listen to their tales of woe. The lies will include exaggerations of real human faults. They will make it appear that the victim's honest errors in judgment and their mistakes were intentional attempts at harming the narce. The narce will also mislead people as to their own abilities and actions. Their goal is to make themselves appear as the *superior person who did the victim a favor by staying with them for as long as they did.*

Love Bombing: The "fun" part of the narce relationship where the victim seems to be on top of the world. The narce is fun, funny, giving, devoted, joyful, and makes the victim feel so very loved. The victim thinks that they have found their perfect soul mate, the love of their life, even while the narce is plotting to discard the victim. The goal of the love bombing is to rope the victim in so fully that the victim trusts the narce completely. During this fun part of the relationship, which never happens again, the narce is figuring out what makes the victim tick. The narce wants to learn all about the victim's life, habits, hopes, dreams ambitions, and everything else they can discover. In return, the narce gives little or no information to the victim. The narce may seem to be sharing things about themselves, too, during this phase of the relationship. But when the victim looks back and thinks about it, they realize that the narce gave very few, if any, true facts about their own lives and inner thoughts. This is yet another control method the narce uses right from the beginning.

Love, Empathic: This is a normal and healthy state of a human being. We are engineered to give, receive, and thrive in love. Empathic love is a genuine and honest feeling that drives one to get to know another person both inside and out. Empathy is critical to a healthy love relationship. If both parties do not understand or sincerely seek to understand how the other person feels, then there is no real relationship. Empathetic love is two-way and sincere. It is real, it is kind and each partner supports the other in their dreams and ambitions. There are no selfish ulterior motives, there is no desire to use the other person to get this or that. In an empathetic love relationship, each person cares for the other and neither is trying to take control of the other. This is not to say that the relationship will be perfect, but it is to say that equal partners will seek to help one another in all ways. Each will be sincerely happy to watch the other progress and have their time in the spotlight.

Love, Narcissistic: This is an abnormal and unhealthy state for a human being. We are engineered to love, but when love gets twisted, it is quite damaging. Narce love is a disingenuous expression of feeling. While a narce is driven to get to know another person both inside and out, it is for selfish purposes. Empathy is critical to a healthy love relationship. If both parties do not understand or sincerely seek to understand how the other person feels, then there is no real relationship. With a narce, there is no two-way reciprocation. The love is not real and the relationship is based on the narce getting their supply. The narce supports the other in only pre-approved dreams and ambitions that the narce wants their partner to have. There are only selfish ulterior motives and a desire to use the victim to get this or that. The narce will seek their own benefit first, second and last. The only benefit the *narce* seeks for the other is that which is beneficial to the narce, i.e. *"I would love to see you pass your dental board, honey because I know you really want to become a DDS. (And boy, will l love the money you will bring in! Plus, if I get tired of you and divorce you, half is mine and I don't have to put up with you anymore!")*

Mask: The narce will always wear a mask. The narce does not care about the truth, they do not care if they harm, they do not care about anything but getting their supply. They get their supply by taking charge and controlling their environment and the people in it. They will change masks and appearances, opinions, and ideas to suit the situation, no matter how they must contradict themselves, deceive, and lie. The narce must never be trusted, *especially when they are behaving in a very friendly way.* The only time they are friendly is when they are trying to learn something about you, get something from you, or maybe they are gloating. Being friendly or pretending to have empathy for you is a way to try to hide their negative opinion of you. They want you to think nothing but the best of them.

Mental/Emotional Illness: This is not a complete guide to what causes the narce to behave as they do and it is not fair to try and discuss in this book whether or not the narce is mentally/emotionally ill. But it is fair to say that the narce's behavior is not "normal". It is also fair to say that the victim likely will need some help to get over the destruction that the narce caused them. The narce obviously needs some kind of help or guidance themselves, but will almost never seek it. They don't believe for a minute that anything is wrong with them or their behavior. They paint the victim in a bad light to keep the attention on the faults of the victim and off of their own flaws. Exposure of a narce's weakness is an affront to their false self. Exposure will always cause narcissistic injury.

Mirroring: This term refers to retaliation by the victim. Out of desperation, the victim will sometimes try to mimic the narce's abusive behavior to get their attention. They hope that the narce will feel bad about their own behavior when they see it played out in front of them. They hope that the narce will understand how badly the victim must feel when the narce treats them that way. There are several problems with this thinking: The victim will not be as good at the abuse as the narce, so they cannot play the part as well. Then the narce will never forgive or forget the mirrored behavior. They will constantly bring this up to the victim as in "I still remember the time…" and they will not hesitate to tell others all about it. The narce will use this as a weapon to punish the victim and strengthen their case against them. Mirroring is never a good idea simply because it does not work and it diminishes the character of the victim because they stooped as low as the narce. They committed acts of abuse toward the narce. Not only that but in the end, the narce does not care about repairing the relationship and this is a wasted effort.

Narce: A term coined by the author to abbreviate the word "narcissist". Most authors and speakers use the term 'narc', but that term also has the meaning of being a "rat" or "snitch". It is a street slang term that is short for "narcotics officer". For this reason, the author uses "narce".

Narcissistic Injury: It may sound as though this is an injury caused by a narcissist. It is actually injury *felt by* the narce. We cannot possibly list all of the things that can cause narce injury. Just remember that the façade, the False Self, the narce ego, or simply put, the self-proclaimed superiority of the narce is a cover. This is a fragile shell that covers a gooey center of fear and insecurity inside the narce. The narce fears this being discovered because of their feelings of inferiority. Any accomplishment made by the victim in the presence of the narce is a narcissistic injury. The narce feels that another person's success is offensive. The narce feels diminished by successes that are not their own. When one's ego is that large, there always going to be a perception of offense. The 'offenses' are always taken personally and injure the narce deeply!

New Darkness: This is a state of mind that a narce may create within a victim. In particular, this may happen when the victim tries to defend themselves against narce abuse. To create the new darkness, there are specific steps that must be taken. (1.) The victim wants to show the narce how awful it feels to be abused, and takes action. (2.) The victim does the same abusive things back to the narce. (3.) The narce uses that abuse as an example of the victim's imperfection. (4.) The narce then tells the victim that have just proved that they are capable of being just as dark as the narce is, so the victim is no better off than the narce. (5.) The victim now sees themselves as living in a new state of darkness. (6.) The narce perpetuates this idea and forever uses it against the victim. When the victim leaves the narce and looks back, they may wonder at the dark things they were doing. The victim needs to take it easy on themselves and renew their light. Many of the dark things the victim did were under the influence of the narce. They probably did a lot of things to please the narce and ease the abuse.

No Contact: This a condition that the victim needs to initiate as soon as possible. While it is true that some factors may affect the totality of going no contact, the victim must minimize contact to the highest degree possible. Children belonging to both the narce and the victim may cause the victim to contact the narce because of child support and custody. In these cases, an attorney or social worker will have options that will allow victim-to-narce communication without actually talking to the person. *Online options of chatting that is closely monitored are a good option.* As much as it goes against normal desires to communicate sensibly, sensible communication is impossible for the narcissist. The sooner the victim accepts that they are the prey and the narce is the predator with no normal affection, the sooner they can go no contact and begin the healing process.

Overt Narcissist: This type of narce is flamboyant and very outgoing, complimenting others and telling them how great they look, etc. They will appear to be the most wonderful person in the world, and people will think they are great. Then when they get home, they will act like their true selves and become abusive. Then when the victim reaches out for help, others will not believe the victim, because everyone will know what a "wonderful person" the narce is. They will know with their whole mind and heart that the narce "could not possibly be the problem". The victim will not be heard and believed in their immediate social group and maybe not even in their family circle. The flamboyant narce will always try to ruin anyone who does not buy into their false self.

Peer: This is a term the author uses in place of "victim" to describe a person who has overcome their narce abuser. The victim becomes a peer the very moment they pull themselves away from narce and engage them as an equal person with equal rights. This term is not intended to suggest that the victim has healed, but it is to suggest the victim is no longer under the narce's thumb. The peer becomes such by throwing off narce control and engaging in life on their own terms, working to heal from the abuse.

Pig Wrestling: This refers to any argument or disagreement with a narce. The victim cannot win an argument with the narce. The narce will instead draw the victim into the noxious pigsty of their illogic, self-aggrandizement, and immaturity. There, the narce has no boundaries and no limits to what they say or do. They have no limits because *the narce believes that everything they say or do is right. After all, they, who can do wrong, are the ones saying and doing it!* Thus, the narce drags the victim through their pigsty and soundly beats them by a home-field advantage. The victim cannot win the rigged game because the victim has rules they live by, as normal people should. Since there are some things victims will not say or do, they will lose against the no-holds-barred narce. This is why the victim must go in contact as much as possible with the narce.

Playing the Victim: The narce will always, without fail, play the victim. The narce will always make it look like they are the injured party. It will not matter what kind of relationship it is. It could be at work, a social relationship, a romantic interest… it simply does not matter. The narce will always manipulate people to gain support. The supporters are being played by the narce. The supporters will always say that the narce is a wonderful person and could not be the problem. The narce will use these people to crush the victim's reputation. Most often, the narce will claim that the victim is doing to them what they are actually doing to the victim. This is also a type of "deflecting".

Poking the Bruise: The narce will make personal remarks about their victim. Nothing is left out. They will attack the victim's physical appearance, upbringing, the victim's family, financial condition, lack of education, etc. They will use anything that they know bothers the victim. For example, they may claim: "You grew up poor and ignorant because your parents are poor and ignorant." The victim will try to not respond because they don't want to fight. The narce will keep making that same remark or alluding to it in some subtle way, over and over. They will keep this up, knowing that it will eventually upset the victim. When the victim finally becomes upset and tries, justly, to defend themselves, the narce will say something like "See how unreasonable you are?" Or worse yet, if the upset occurs in a public setting, "See everyone, why I can't deal with him/her?" Note that the narce will not hesitate to make a public scene if they feel like it.

Projection: This is a favorite technique among narces. They will inevitably use this. The *narce* will absolutely project onto the victim the things that the narce themselves are doing. In other words, if the narce is doing it, they will blame the victim for it. If the narce was an overspender, they will blame the victim for poor life/business management skills and an inability to handle money. If the narce has an ill temper, they will "poke the bruise" of the victim in front of others until the victim displays irritation, and then they will "show everyone how unreasonable" the victim is. In short, the victim will always get the blame for the failures and disasters that the narce themselves caused. It will be a game of "I'm not the one doing this…*they* are." This is in the same vein as "deflection". This technique is different, though, because it is used in front of other people to paint a picture of the victim. Think of "projection" as the narce projecting a movie about the victim before an audience.

Think of "deflection" as the narce immediately casting behavior back at the victim with a mirror.

Religious Narcissism: Religion may be one of the favorite tools of the narce because people want to believe in a Higher Power of some kind to make sense of their lives. We see many examples of religion being used as an abusive tool all over the world. When a narce adopts religion, it does not become a better person. It is to learn how to use that religion as a tool to control people. They will use their religion to elevate themselves to grand heights, so that other people will admire, and perhaps even "worship" the narce. The narce will try to somehow convince the group that they are the one who knows all that the others need to know. They will claim that they are somehow enlightened and must be obeyed without question. This can happen in individual homes, friendships, romances, and so on. The group may be as small as two or as large as the number of people who are willing to become believers. The narce will often create small communities of "believers" to follow them within a church. Beware of religious narces because they can quickly become very dangerous, especially if they actually believe they are the agents of a Higher Power. *NOTE: Understand that not all religious leaders are narces. There truly are enlightened people who want to improve the world around them. There is nothing wrong with seeking and following truly wise and enlightened counsel.*

Revenge, Empathic: A healthy person will not seek revenge against the narce once the relationship hits the rocks. The type of person who becomes a narce's victim is a genuinely sincere and nice person. However, for their own good, they must end the relationship. They must *sever themselves from the narce and then set out to become their best self.* This is the best "revenge" that the victim can get, even though they are not looking for revenge. The narce spent a lot of time and effort to break the other person and make them believe they were nothing without the narce. Being proven wrong is one of the things that drives the narce crazy! The victim does not wish to hurt the narce, but the healthiest thing they can do is the same thing that "injures" the narce. Remember that narcissistic injury is not caused by shame or guilt, but it is caused by a loss of supply. Narces are highly offended and injured at the successes of their victim because this shows that the narce was wrong about the victim and the narce is no longer in the spotlight.

Revenge, Narcissistic: Know that the narce will continually seek revenge on anyone who they perceive as having caused them injury. The targets of revenge are anyone who has caused the narce some form of perceived pain or hurt. Narce injuries are perceived in the mind of the narce and are felt very deeply by the narce. The narce has a fragile ego rooted in deep-seated insecurities. The narce was likely raised in a deeply shame-based style that caused these deep injuries. The narce is constantly seeking to keep their pain hidden, but when someone disagrees with them it triggers that pain. Then they will invariably lash out against whoever caused that pain because the narce believes that they should not suffer. They believe that they are above suffering and that *anyone who causes them pain will be taught a lesson.*

Sabotage: The narce can never look bad. They can never be the ones at fault. The only way that narce can claim all of the attention, praise, honors, and glory for themselves is to take it away from other people. They do this by making others look really bad. They will find the faults, weaknesses, and foibles of others and put them on display. They will actively do things that will destroy the others' honest efforts. For instance, in a business deal, the narce may block the efforts of a victim to get a business loan, causing needed finances to fall through. Then the narce will say the victim failed to procure financing, making the victim look bad. Then they will take the victim's idea, use it to prosper, and claim the credit. If the victim objects, the narce will point at the victim's failure and say that they were incapable.

Scorched Earth: A scorched earth policy is sometimes used by enemies at war. The vanquished peoples' land is burned and all the buildings, factories, homes, and so on are destroyed. Farms are tilled under and the soil is ruined so they cannot grow crops or livestock. Many times, they will "scorch the earth" by using poisons to pollute the land and even the water. The point is to render the land useless to anyone, ever again. To do such a thing is about as dastardly as it gets. We must understand that this is what the narce wants to do to the victim. They want to ruin the victim's reputation, destroy their social circle, ruin their family relationships, drain them of their money and financial opportunities, and so on. The fact is that once the narce is through with the victim, particularly in a serious domestic relationship, the narce wants to ruin the victim. They may even try to get rid of the victim by killing them or having them killed. If murder is not in the cards, then they will do all they can to make the victim unfit for anyone else to have them. The more the victim suffers, the better.

Scorpion Effect: This is about the fable of *The Scorpion and the Frog* which can be found in a Google search. The moral of the story is that a narce, no matter how convincing they may sound to the contrary, is always dangerous. They will harm both their victim and themselves. Then they will blame the victim for that harm with an attitude of "It is just my nature. You should have known better than to get involved with me."

Silent Treatment: This is a method of control that involves the total disregard of the victim. It is a very simple thing and yet quite cruel. It is often used in domestic situations where it is the most effective. The silent treatment involves simply shutting down all communication with the victim while remaining in the home, workplace, church, or other proximity. The narce will not respond to the victim verbally, or even look in the victim's direction. When the victim is empathic, they see this as a problem they need to solve. They want to fix the problem because they believe they must have done something wrong. They are willing to correct whatever they did and will make pleas to the narce for communication. During the silence, emotional and physical intimacy will also be denied to the victim, but the narce is getting supply from others. The supply can come from texting, social media, events the narce attends alone, or in extreme cases, cheating/infidelity. The victim, on the other hand, will be left alone without any support during the silent treatment.

Smear Campaign: The narce will always make sure to paint the victim in the worst possible light. They will present the victim's human flaws and errors exponentially out of context. They will draw innocent people into narce's fantasy about how much they were wronged in the business deal, the friendship, the love affair, the dating relationship, etc. No relationship is ever sacred to the narce and all boundaries will be violated. The narce will often smear the victim during the relationship to prepare for a discard.

Social Abuse: The narce will always abuse the victim in social circles, either behind the victim's back or right out in the open. Often, they will do both. The narce will do little things like correct the victim in public at the dinner table or during some other activity. They will talk over their victim in a conversation, blocking them from having a say. They will often leave the victim alone, while they mingle. In their extended social and family circle, the narce will commit even bigger abuses like deciding who the victim may have as friends and whether or not the victim's family should be around at all. The goal of the narce is to isolate the victim by erecting barriers to rob the victim of all support in a breakup. This is particularly easy to do when there is a language barrier in place that might prevent the victim from communicating for themselves, such as in a multilingual social setting.

Stockholm Syndrome: This is an authentic, recognized psychological problem that is named after the famous kidnapping of Patty Hearst. Hearst began to develop positive feelings for her captor's cause and actually helped them rob banks. She described it as being "brainwashed". The syndrome develops when the abused sees the abuser as "not so bad" because the abuser gives some small concessions now and then. An example would be the victim thinking "These kidnappers may have me tied up in a chair, but they *do* give me food and water." These concessions cause the victim to start accepting the abuser as a good person. Then they believe the abuser has their best interests at heart. Soon, the victim will follow the abuser no matter how they are treated. They may even join in the abuser's practices. This is closely linked to trauma bonding and "new darkness".

Stoic/Stoicism: We may think of stoicism as being strong and silent. In this case, though, stoicism is part of the victim's recovery. Becoming stoic means *the victim decides they will become their very best self despite the* narce. The victim will not give in to the narce and will not allow the narce back into their life. The victim will keep the narce far away. If narce must show up, the victim will not speak any words other than what is necessary for business. The victim is no longer a victim. They will not let the narce stop them from having happiness, peace, good friendships, etc. Note that "gray rocking" is a great example of a stoic practice.

Stonewalling: This is a narcissistic method of abuse. It is related to the 'silent treatment', but is not as quiet. It is deeply dismissive, yes, but it may involve more communication than the silent treatment. Stonewalling will involve some recognition of the victim but without any meaningful communication. The narce may grunt at the victim as a response to a question. They may say "Yes, yes," and disregard the victim entirely. Or they may nod but not pay attention. The short answers or sounds they make are used to convey the message that one was heard (but not listened to.) That way, if asked, the narce can get away with saying that they did not ignore the victim. They simply cannot understand why the victim is so upset. This may be a type of gaslighting because the narce is sending an unclear message so they can say "(The victim) did not understand me correctly," if someone calls them out on it.

Superiority: The narce believes that they are superior to everyone else around them. They honestly believe that they are better than anyone and deserve everything that they can squeeze out of the victim. They believe that the victim should have no attention or praise because the narce is the only one who deserves it. Not only that, but the victim doesn't deserve to have an opinion unless it matches narce's opinion. They believe that all they do is right simply because they are the ones doing it, and they are never wrong. This is a hard thing for a normal person to accept about the narce, but it is the absolute truth.

Supply: Narcissistic supply is a term that is still under debate as to its precise definition. Simply put, the supply is whatever the narce is getting from other people. It could be a feeling of superiority. It could be that they get a thrill out of watching the victim suffer. It could many things. Whatever the supply is, once the victim stops becoming a source of it for the narce, they are discarded like week-old garbage. The narce will think nothing of it. Anyone around the narce is there for supply and no other reason. Anyone not providing supply will not be permitted to remain in the narce's circle. They will reject anyone who is not providing some form of supply, even if it's simple amusement.

Toxic Personality: When something is "toxic", it is poisonous, dangerous, and deadly. One of the hardest things for the victim to face is the fact that someone they genuinely love is toxic. Empaths in particular cannot comprehend the depth, height, and breadth of the narce's toxicity. It often seems impossible for the victim to understand how badly they have been duped. The normal, empathetic person cannot comprehend it because they cannot believe that "people are actually like that." It seems impossible. But the sooner the victim wraps their head around this and accepts that the narce is *truly that bad*, the sooner the victim can heal.

Trauma Bonding: This is a perceived need of a victim to have the narce abuser's love. The victim may remember the kind of things the abuser used to do for them. These kindnesses are the "love bombs" that the narce dropped on the victim in the beginning. The abused will crave that euphoric love once again, believing that the narce "still loves them deep inside" because they leave "bread crumbs". The narce will know this and will also do bigger favors for the victim during the "hoovering" to keep the victim sucked into the narce's circle. The hope for love and affection that will never be again is the bond. That hope is false and as difficult as it is, the victim must learn to abandon that hope. It may be necessary to seek professional help with breaking the trauma bond.

Traumatic Brain Injury: The victim of long-term, narcissistic abuse has learned certain coping mechanisms. Over the long term, narce abuse victims actually suffer alterations in their brain's structure. It has been proven that the constant chaos, fear, gaslighting, lack of support, etc. will cause damage to the victim similar to that suffered by combat veterans. This may sound extreme on the surface, but with a little digging, one will learn that living with a narce is very similar to combat. *The relationship is steeped in conflict, unpredictability, threats to one's safety and security, an overworked adrenal response, sudden changes in life status, and constant fearful living...*all of this is similar to one who has suffered in combat. Traumatic brain damage is quite possible and is quite real in narce relationships. The victim is hereby encouraged to seek professional/medical help to get through this. The good news is that the changes or "damage" to the brain were triggered by a survival response. With time and treatment, the victim can get better. The most critical thing that can be said here is that *it is not the victim's imagination and it is not something that is 'cured' quickly. The damage is just as real as damage to a combat veteran or a head trauma victim.*

Vampirism: We are all familiar with the vampires of the horror movies and TV shows. We learn how the vampire is desperately thirsty for blood, which it drinks from the veins of its victims. Well, the narce is desperately thirsty, too. Like the vampire who would die from a lack of blood, the narce will die from a lack of "supply". The narce will drain their victim of all they have, including their precious reserve of life's energy. This is particularly true if the victim is an empath. The narce has no internal reserves of love or self-respect, so they will get what they crave at a very high cost to others. One of the symptoms victims complain of, particularly when getting out of the narce relationship is how "exhausted" they are. The narce will leave their victim emotionally, financially, socially, and spiritually exhausted.

Word Salad: This is about a narce's conversation. They will speak to the victim in the kindest of terms. They will use scholarly references and name-dropping of authorities or famous people to look really impressive. The narce will tell you how much they give, how great they are, and will use pedantic speech and fancy words. All of this is a smoke screen to cover ineptitude. They will try to impress people and create the best possible image for themselves. They often use word salad to avoid any topic at hand that may not be in their favor, such as a flaw of theirs. The narce will not mean anything that they say during word salad. They may not even know the true meaning of the words they are using. They certainly do not mean these impressive things from their hearts. Many of these words are platitudes or even quotes from wise men or holy people which do not solve the problem. They may not even apply to the situation. The word salad is used as a smokescreen to confuse the victim and elevate the narce. Word salad increases the fog and confusion which is such an important part of the narce's game. Remember that they thrive on confusion, drama, and chaos, not on solving problems and creating clarity.

Author's Note: If you have read this book this far, you have done so for a reason. I would personally urge you to immediately seek out help if you even slightly believe that you are, or were once a victim of narcissistic abuse. Don't hesitate, GET HELP.

As a starting point, I would suggest going to Dr. Les Carter's videos on YouTube. He seems to be a very kindly man and this is a good place to start your journey. You may even want to involve clergy or spiritual advisors if you are at all a religious or spiritual person. Take your time and find a professional counselor trained in narcissistic abuse and/or a support group to help guide you on your new journey to discover who you really are.

www.ingramcontent.com/pod-product-compliance
Lightning Source LLC
Chambersburg PA
CBHW070516160726
48003CB00004B/1594